Arctic Summer

Richard Vaughan

Arctic Summer

Birds in North Norway

Anthony Nelson

First published in 1979 by Anthony Nelson Limited,
7 St John's Hill, Shrewsbury, SY1 1JE, Shropshire, England.

ISBN 0 904614 01 8

Photographs by Richard Vaughan

Designed by Alan Bartram and printed in Great Britain
by Livesey Limited, Shrewsbury, Shropshire.

Contents

TO MY FRIENDS IN THE VARANGER PENINSULA

Introduction

Like so many others, I had for long felt the spell of the far north and dreamed of a bird-watching visit to Lapland or Iceland. But it was not until I arrived in Yorkshire and met Henry Bunce that my plans finally crystallised. Henry not only found time from his job in Hull to be the East Riding's official bird recorder; he has also over the years become a passionate enthusiast for Sweden. He is one of the very few English ornithologists who knows the language; he has acquired an intimate knowledge of the country, its birds and its bird-watchers. It was he who one day pointed out to me on the map, as worth a visit, a place much further north than the northern tip of his beloved Sweden – the Varanger Peninsula, in the county of Finnmark, Norway. In May 1971 I asked the then Vice-Chancellor of the University of Hull, where I am employed as a historian, for the first leave of absence I had ever applied for, and the Registrar was subsequently able to inform me that I had been officially granted this leave in order to study the birds of East Finnmark. It was to extend from 5 June to 22 July 1972. The University authorities had played their part, but it was my colleagues in the Department of History who would enable me to be away during what is the university teacher's busiest time, the examination month of June; which happens to coincide with the almost explosively short breeding season of the birds of the Arctic.

In the past I had made expeditions to places whose birds were virtually unknown and which were entirely without resident bird-watchers. The massif of Monte Maiella, for example, in the Central Apennines. This venture was something quite different. After all, the Varanger Peninsula boasts an active branch of the Norwegian Ornithologists' Union or Norsk Ornitologisk Forening; there is a bird-watcher in every village, almost, from Varangerbotn to Vadsø. More than a dozen papers have been published in recent years containing observations on the birds of Finnmark, and the Varanger Peninsula has annually, since 1965, attracted increasing numbers of ornithological visitors from Sweden, Germany, Holland, England and even France. In 1971 Svein Haftorn's magnificent work *Norges fugler* with its detailed distribution maps and wealth of recent data added very substantially to our already considerable knowledge of Varanger birds. In spite of all this, however, the information available so far is fragmentary. Most of the visiting bird-watchers who have published their Varanger notes were in the Peninsula for a few days only. Most of the resident bird-watchers live on the southern shore of the Peninsula which is the area most often worked by visiting ornithologists. The purpose of my investigation was to try to cover more ground and to do so over a longer period of time. The purpose of this book is to present a portrait of the varied bird life of this still largely unspoilt and even unexplored region.

Why the Varanger Peninsula? Though it has a wild beauty all its own, its landscape cannot compare with the spectacular mountain or fjord scenery of many other parts of Norway. Its bird life is by no means unique. But it does contain one of the largest areas of so-called tundra in Scandinavia; it is almost the most north-easterly and indisputably the most easterly part of that peninsula; and it does form a geographical unity. It has the added advantage that the English ornithologist and egg-collector, H. M. S. Blair, spent several summers there in the 1920's and 1930's and published an exhaustive paper on the local birds in 1936 which would form an ideal base line for my own researches. But perhaps the greatest advantage of the Varanger Peninsula is one of communications. It is traversed by roads which cross its wild interior in one place and nearly encircle its coast. In this respect it is much better served than North Norway's other great peninsulas, which are in fact considerably smaller, such as neighbouring Nordkinn or remote Svaerholt, further west and entirely roadless.

The Varanger Peninsula then, could be worked by car, and what could be more convenient than our Volkswagen motor caravan? In it I could go where I pleased and sleep where I pleased. There was ample room for the warm clothes that were thought necessary; the several boxes of tinned food; a small library of ornithological reference works; sufficient camping equipment, including a light weight tent to make it possible to move away from the roads; and, above all, the photographic equipment. For I took with me three miniature cameras – two Nikkormats and a Nikon – five lenses ranging in focal length from 50 to 1,000 mm, four tripods, two electronic flash guns and more besides, not to mention four portable hides.

The months before departure were taken up with planning and preparation. Inventories were made of gear and provisions and other necessaries. The literature was searched and a list of Varanger birds drawn up. Letters of enquiry were sent to, and friendly and helpful replies received, from the Swedish bird photographer and friend of Henry Bunce, Gösta Håkansson, who had been to the Varanger Peninsula several times, the Norwegian ornithologists Einar Brun of the Tromsø Museum and E. K. Barth of Oslo University, and the leading resident ornithologist in the Varanger Peninsula, Jostein Grastveit. This last one showed me a letter he had received from a Dutch ornithologist he had never met. The envelope was addressed in English 'to the best-known bird-watcher in Vadsø, Norway.' Last, but not least, I made great efforts to convert my not very profound reading knowledge of the Scandinavian languages into spoken

Norwegian. I listened to the Norwegian tapes in the University's Language Laboratory and was astonished to hear a Norwegian academic speaking English better than most Englishmen. But I disappointed my mentors there by breaking off the course to take lessons with a Norwegian au-pair girl from Trondheim called Trude Olsen. She thought I was crazy to spend my time watching birds and crazy too, to visit such a remote area of her country. Why learn Norwegian in any case? There was nobody at all in the Varanger Peninsula, according to Trude. Even if I did meet with other human beings there, they would most probably be Lapps, who would speak English. Nonetheless, she bore with me politely and patiently while I falteringly travestied her beautiful language.

My indebtedness and gratitude to the many Norwegians who befriended and helped me is expressed in the dedication of this book. In five all too short weeks they gained my admiration and respect and I learned to love one of the furthest outposts of their superb country. This book, the outcome of my experiences, is a personal statement about birds; but also, less obviously perhaps, though in many ways more profoundly, a statement about Norway.

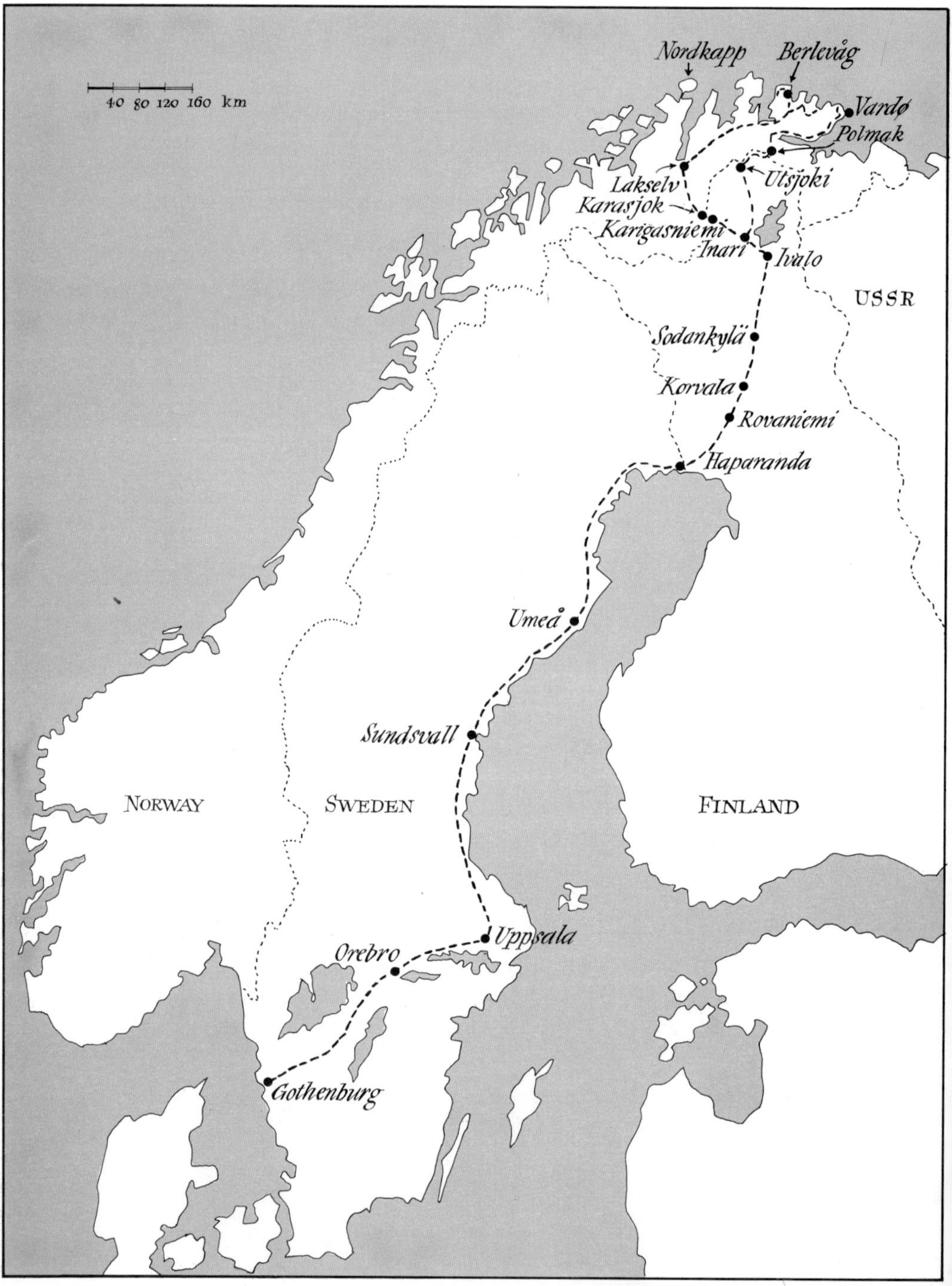

40 80 120 160 km
Nordkapp
Berlevåg
Vardø
Polmak
Lakselv
Utsjoki
Karasjok
Karigasniemi
Inari
Ivalo
USSR
Sodankylä
Korvala
Rovaniemi
Haparanda
Umeå
Sundsvall
NORWAY
SWEDEN
FINLAND
Uppsala
Orebro
Gothenburg

The Journey

I

There was no difficulty at all in settling the most expeditious and practicable route from my home town of Hull to the Varanger Peninsula. After crossing the mud-brown Humber in one of the world's last coal-fired paddle-wheel ferryboats still in regular service, and driving the twenty miles or so to Immingham, I embarked at about 1530 hours on the afternoon of Sunday 4 June in the blue and white Tor Anglia. The ship towered like some huge hotel above the flat green pastures with cows browsing in them which fringed the Humber, contrasting forcefully with the tall blue cranes, the container boxes, and the oil storage tanks, of the docks. The North Sea crossing from Immingham to Gothenburg (Göteborg) in Sweden takes about twenty-five hours. On this occasion it was accomplished in superb weather throughout the daylight hours of 5 June; the ship gliding smoothly through a calm flat sea, deep blue when the sun was behind you; glassy and scintillating when you faced it. At last we reached the smooth rounded rock skerries outside Gothenburg and the scent of resin from innumerable pines wafted across from the land just as the ship was joined by the first (Scandinavian) lesser black-backed gulls.

I had resolved to journey onwards from Gothenburg without unnecessary intermission of any kind in order to reach the Varanger Peninsula as early as possible. I knew that the ruffs would cease their lekking there about the middle of June and that time was short for other species too. I was impelled by a feeling of urgency, a sense of mission, an overwhelming need to reach my distant destination as quickly as possible. The long drive through three-quarters of Sweden and half of Finland was an adventure, yes, but also a hard and at times tedious grind. I carried it through in a headlong rush, though without driving fast; indeed, without even exceeding the speed limits, and allowing myself ample time to rest at intervals during the day and sleep at night. Delays were fortunately minimal. Lost in Gothenburg at the outset, the man I stopped to ask the way spoke perfect English, addressed me as sir, and obligingly and quite spontaneously climbed into the front passenger seat and insisted on accompanying me until I was back on my route.

Compared to much of England, driving conditions in Sweden, even relatively crowded South Sweden, are admirable. In this motorists' paradise I had no difficulty in driving 192 miles in just under four hours, after I passed through the Gothenburg customs office at 1800 hours. After a brief halt in a pine-surrounded layby, I was off again in the dawn of a beautiful warm summer day, driving for mile after mile through the scented pine forest; then along, though usually out of sight of, a deep blue Baltic Sea. At Sundsvall on its creek I parked the car and walked round the town's tree-lined and crowded main square with its fountains. Everybody seemed to be out strolling in the sun. At last, after the longest and most beautiful single day's drive in my life, I arrived at Umeå, the mouth of the River Ume, at 1745 hours, some fourteen hours after setting out, having driven 485 miles that day. I was more than half-way up the Gulf of Bothnia after covering about half the length of Sweden. It was 6 June. The daffodils were in flower in Umeå, but the tulips were still in bud, I turned in at 2100 hours in the camp-site above the town. It was still, calm and quiet. An immense golden sun hung in the sky above a horizon of endless pine forest.

All morning, next day, for five hours between 0810 hours and 1322 hours, I drove north along the shores of the Gulf of Bothnia before stopping for lunch just short of Haparanda at the head of the Gulf, the last place in Sweden on my route. I had covered a further 244 miles of the European Road No 4 (E4), which runs from Lisbon through Madrid, Basel, Copenhagen and Stockholm, then round the northern end of the Gulf of Bothnia to end at Helsinki. Much of this stretch of road was gently undulating with a few slight curves here and there. Sometimes the fir trees were close up on either side, almost overhanging the road, usually they were set back from the road, separated from it by a steep bank and ditch. There was birch forest too, the trees just coming into leaf, and occasional shallow lakes and bogs where the landscape seemed to have a touch of the Arctic. River after river was crossed, the smaller ones with sepia-coloured or even almost black, water, brilliantly sparkling in the sun, with white bubbles on the surface and, in some cases, banks carpeted with marsh marigolds in full bloom. An osprey flew over the car. The sun shone all day long from a blue sky. I had seen Sweden and her marvellous coniferous forests at their loveliest.

By 1735 hours on Wednesday, 7 June, when I reached the lakeside camp-site at Korvala in Finland, I had driven 472 miles that day, having crossed the Arctic Circle north of Rovaniemi. When you enter Finland over the River Tornio a policeman politely waves you into a layby near the customs house. A charming girl with a lapel badge labelled 'Tourist Guide' asks you in English if there is anything she can do for you and wishes you *bon voyage*. When I asked her about passports and Green Cards she waved me on with the words 'Oh! This is our free country!' Twenty-four hours later I entered Norway at the remote village of Polmak, halting at two simple notices, one saying *Norge*, the other *Toll*, on the frontier. The authorities here were even more casual: a mere wave of an arm from inside the customs house was the only formality. I drove on into Norway.

The Korvala camp-site was not yet officially open, though it was 7 June. I shared it with two German families. The temperature of the lake was 56°F. One of the Germans had a permit to fish for salmon in it, but the wild beauty of this forest-surrounded lake was a tiny bit tarnished by the conditions imposed on his sport. He could only fish between 1900 and 2100 hours, at a daily cost of 10 Finnish marks (£1). His fish were to be inspected by the owners and an additional charge made of 10 marks for every kilo of fish caught!

Thursday 8 June began cold and dull. I drove northwards through Finland under a grey sky, setting off from Korvala at 0630 hours, halting briefly for breakfast, and covering 237 miles before stopping for lunch at 1330 hours just short of the last place in Finland, Utsjoki. At one point the road suddenly grew disconcertingly and immensely wide; it was just that for a mile or so it formed the central strip of a tarmac airfield runway. Between Ivalo and Inari the road was, to put it as kindly as possible, under construction. After Inari, whose lake with its myriad pine-clad islands was still ice-covered, the road was mostly quite good though narrow, with frequent passing places, one always in sight of another. Here was a barren, desolate, stony upland, its birch trees not yet in leaf, nor even showing buds, its pines thinning out and often devastated by fire. Here and there were ice-covered lakes in hollows; snow drifts were frequent. Sometimes a superb vista opened up westwards, towards the Norwegian mountains which looked entirely snow-covered, a vista whose immense sweep took in in its foreground the splendid Finnish Kevo National Park. Traffic all day was almost non-existent. Repeatedly I found myself aware of the uncanny emptiness of the landscape, almost ill at ease. How curious it was to stop for lunch in a layby and have nobody driving past you along the road!

It was at 1715 hours on Thursday 8 June that I finally arrived at my destination: Nesseby in the Varanger Peninsula. The mileometer recorded that I had driven 1,350 miles since leaving the Tor Anglia at Gothenburg almost exactly three days before. Since my lunch-break near Utsjoki on this last day I had stopped briefly by the majestic River Tana, whose frozen surface is used as a motor road in winter, to admire the jumbled blocks of ice piled high along its banks. Proud producer, in former days, of the world's largest-ever salmon, weighing over 80 lb, the River Tana is now over fished and its salmon stocks are sadly depleted. Then my route turned eastwards and led out of the valley of the Tana over a sepia-brown birch-forested upland and down to the shores of the Varanger Fjord. At Nesseby, where I sat in the car with brilliant sunshine streaming in through the open side-door, and a bitingly cold east wind outside, my long journey was over. Phalaropes were flitting over and feeding round a grassy pool a few yards from the car. It was high time to start looking at birds.

My return journey from the Varanger Peninsula between 15 and 20 July was almost as rapid and equally uneventful. I ended, as I had started, my sojourn in the Varanger Peninsula, with a visit to Nesseby: once again, as before, a harsh east wind was blowing in brilliant sunlight. I allowed myself additional time on the return journey in order to drive along the spectacular mountain road over the 1,000 feet high Ifjord Fell to Lakselv at the southern tip, or head, of the Porsanger Fjord, and thence south to Karasjok. The night of 15 July I spent by the shore of the Laksefjord where a magnificent system of raised beaches, tiered in a sweeping semi-circle one above the other, extended high above the sea and the road. Above them was a great cliff of steeply-sloping rocks, worn smooth by the waves of some primeval ocean. But nowhere perhaps is the destroying hand of man more apparent than in this gaunt and desolate rocky landscape, for the raised beaches have in places been quarried almost out of existence for their gravel and sand deposits. As I turned in at 2300 hours the sun dipped behind a cloud in the north-west, turning the fjord below me a brilliant silver, and a distant redwing sang high on the hillside above.

Next day I moved south to Sodankylä in Finland, almost exactly 300 miles away. It was exciting to see pine trees again. Sparse among the still predominant birch north of Karasjok, here they stood thick and tall and intermingled with stately spruces with their drooping branches. I passed from Norway into Finland at Karigasniemi, famed for its bird localities, which include the wader-haunted Mount Ailigas, now perhaps made too accessible by road for the safety of its birds. Sodankylä is little more than a clearing in the pines; the graveyard is actually in the pine forest and the horizon all round is composed of pines. It is a colourful, pleasant little town of wooden houses with a sand martin colony virtually at ground level in the bank of a roadside ditch. The evening of 17 July saw me far down the Gulf of Bothnia, at Umeå again, in splendid sunny weather, and I spent the evening of 18 July exploring the attractive and peaceful university town of Uppsala, with its magnificent brick cathedral, fine castle and modern pedestrian shopping precincts. For the first time in weeks I experienced darkness. Next day, 19 July, I drove across southern Sweden to Gothenburg, arriving in time to swim in that most beautiful of all lakes, on the eastern outskirts of the town, Delsjön. The blue waters of Delsjön with the pines reflected in them in every direction, and its ice-smoothed boulders, seemed to typify the beauty of the Scandinavian countryside. It reminded me that the Varanger Peninsula, where I had spent the last few weeks, was by no means typical, for it lay north of that hallmark of Scandinavian scenery, the seemingly endless forest of pine and spruce.

Bird-watching by the light of the midnight sun: the author in Kibymyr, photographed by Jostein Grastveit.

The Varanger Peninsula

2

Lying as far north as northern Alaska and as far east as Odessa and Cairo, the Varanger Peninsula is Norway's largest peninsula. On the south it is bounded by one of the country's largest fjords, the Varanger Fjord, 118 km long. On the west it is separated from the mainland by the River Tana and the Tana Fjord, both of which lie approximately north-south. Its rugged north-east coast lies open to the Barents Sea. The Varanger Peninsula is about 100 km in length in an east-west direction and some 90 km broad north-south. A high ridge extends intermittently along its length, towering 724 m above the Tana Fjord on the west coast of the peninsula; 618 m high at Hanglefjell some miles south-eastwards; and rising to 637 m in the centre of the peninsula. South of this ridge are three enormous flat rounded fells or low mountains. The best known is the most easterly, Falkefjell, rising to 548 m some 18 km north of Vadsø. The central plateau of the most westerly of these relatively high fells is Sørfjell, rising to 458 m. Though far north of the Arctic Circle, because of the warming influence of the Gulf Stream, which keeps the north coast of Norway ice-free throughout the year, the Varanger Peninsula only barely qualifies as Arctic. The 10°C July isotherm passes just north of it; the northern limit of the birch forest, the so-called tree line, passes through it. Fir trees are nowadays unknown in this region though their roots have been found in bogs along the southern shore of the peninsula.

The county of Finnmark includes the whole northern tip of Norway along with the Varanger Peninsula. It is larger than Denmark. There are three towns, properly speaking, Hammerfest, Vadsø and Vardø. The population, if spread out evenly, would reach a density of about 1.5 persons per square kilometre, as opposed to 11 in Norway as a whole. It includes two substantial minority groups speaking languages of their own, Lapps and Finns. The earliest inhabitants were Lapps; the Norwegians settled on the peninsula at the end of the middle ages and in early modern times; the Finns moved in during the nineteenth century. In the Varanger Peninsula virtually all the permanent houses are on the coast, but the interior is dotted with numerous huts or bungalows, mostly exceedingly ugly, which are used for fishing, skiing and other recreations.

In Vardø, famous as the starting point of the Arctic explorations of two great explorers, the Dutchman Willem Barents and the Norwegian Fridtjof Nansen, and known to seventeenth-century English seamen as Wardhouse, there were 3,471 persons in 1960. In 1944, at the end of the war, much of the Varanger Peninsula had been evacuated, depopulated and devastated by the retreating Germans. Invited to leave their island home and be resettled on the mainland

Top: *The phalarope pool at Nesseby on the shore of the Varanger Fjord.*

Bottom: *Beyond the smooth inclined rock slabs of the north-east face of Hanglefjell is the undulating, lake-strewn, tundra.*

Top: *Spring comes to the fells of the Varanger Peninsula late in the year – there is still plenty of snow about in early June.*

Bottom: *An Arctic tern incubates by the road outside the village of Saltjern.*

opposite in a New Town, the inhabitants of Vardø had elected to stay put. The first castle at Vardø was built in the middle ages; the present star-shaped structure dates from 1738.

Vadsø, on the southern shore of the peninsula, which numbered 3,077 souls in 1960, is the administrative capital of Finnmark County and is dominated by the twin red and white masts of its radio station. The original settlement here was on the offshore island once called Kirkeøya, but in the seventeenth century a church was built on the mainland opposite and houses gradually accumulated round it. By about 1700 the island was deserted and its church demolished. Today the island, called Vadsøya, is linked to the mainland by a wooden bridge. A number of houses have been built on it during this century as well as the airship mast used by Amundsen and Nobile for their Polar flights in 1926 and 1928.

By North Norwegian standards the Varanger Peninsula is well provided with roads. Sections of the road along the south shore from Varangerbotn to Svartnes opposite Vardø were being built towards the close of the nineteenth century. Completed early this century and reckoned one of the oldest motor roads in Norway, this road has recently been largely rebuilt and modernised. The other important road, which crosses the interior of the peninsula from the mouth of the Tana River to Kongsfjord and Berlevåg, with more recent extensions to Store Molvik, Båtsfjord and Syltefjord, was built in 1959. It goes by the rather grand name of Arctic Ocean Highway (Ishavsveien), though much of it is only a narrow ribbon of hard gravel, and the entire inland sector is closed by snow from December to May every year. Transport in winter has recently been revolutionised by the introduction of one or two-man snow-scooters, and by Canadian snowmobiles which were introduced in 1950 and can carry fourteen adult passengers at 50–60 km per hour.

Fishing, of course, is the main industry in the Varanger Peninsula. The wooden racks or poles on which cod and other fishes are hung up to dry are conspicuous in or near all the towns and villages. Agriculture, apart from limited reindeer herding by a few Lapps, is confined in the main to the growing of hay, which is used to feed both cattle and sheep through the long winter. Near Berlevåg, while being driven along the European continent's most northerly mainland road, I was shown the world's most northerly cows. The hayfields are small, fenced and carefully fertilised. The growth of grass is rapid and lush, accelerated by the continuous daylight of the summer months, and hay cutting was in full swing when I left the peninsula in the middle of July. The hay is hung up to dry on parallel wire fences arranged down the middle of the fields. Other crops are sparse indeed, but a number

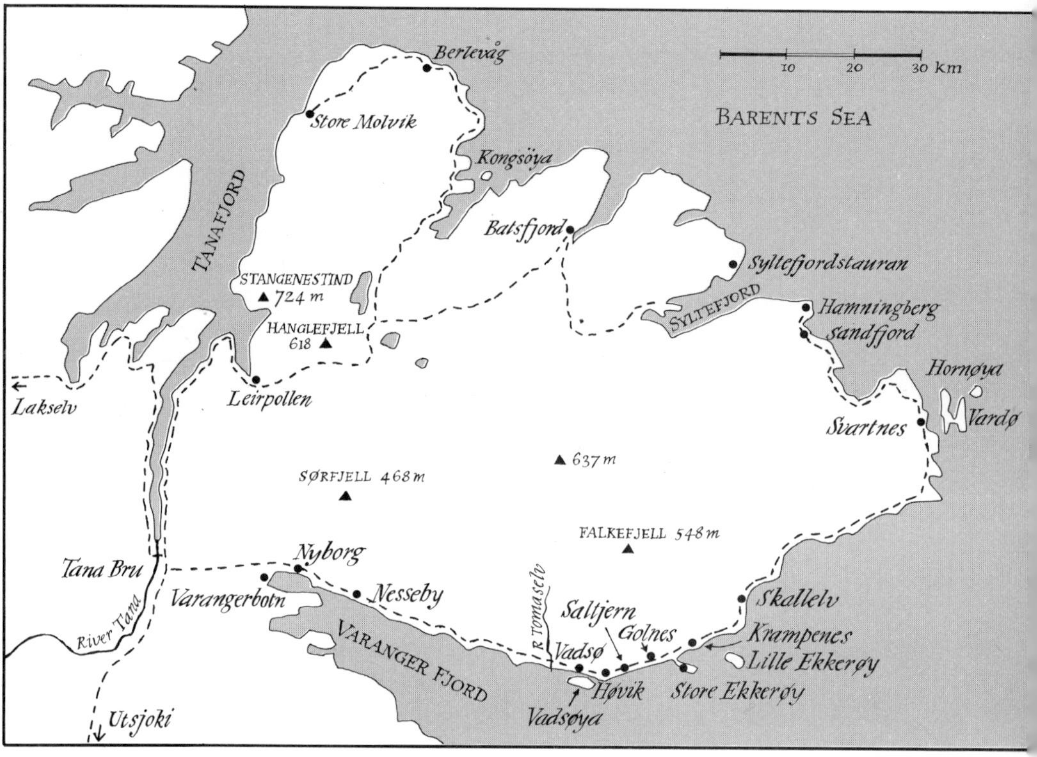

of small potato fields near houses were clearly going to yield useful crops, though only because of careful mulching and fertilisation.

Although there are many fragments of birch and willow scrub scattered throughout low-lying parts of the peninsula, continuous growth of birch is limited to the valleys of its south-western corner, from Vadsø to Leirpollen. Under these trees, which are seldom more than six or at the very most ten metres tall, a most luxuriant growth of flowering plants appears in summer, dominated in places by meadow crane's bill (*Geranium*), but everywhere consisting largely of bilberry (*Vaccinium*). Most of the rest of the Varanger Peninsula can only be described as tundra. A very large part of this treeless, bushless area, including much of the northern half of the peninsula right down to sea level and all land above about 300 m, has no vegetation to speak of apart from a sparse growth of lichen. It is a rock or stone desert: no animals, no birds, no flowers, nothing save jumbled frost-sorted rock fragments. The lower fells are however covered with a patchy growth of dwarf birch (*Betula nana*), which often forms quite large 'bushes' absolutely flat on the ground, lichens, and crowberry (*Empetrum nigrum*). This last is one of the most characteristic plants of the

Varanger Peninsula for it monopolises large areas, especially in the low-lying coastal districts of the southern part of the peninsula, forming extensive crowberry heaths. There is of course no heather in the Varanger Peninsula. Numerous bogs are in badly drained hollows among the fells and along the coast, some of them, especially Kibymyr near Vadsø, are quite extensive. The dominant plant, alongside various species of sedge (*Carex*) and cotton-grass (*Eriophorum*) and some rush (*Juncus*) of many of these bogs, is the cloudberry (*Rubus chamaemorus*), the fruits of which are much prized by the local people.

On average, there are only thirty days in the year when the temperature at Vardø is above 10°C. The average temperature in the warmest month, July, is 8.9°C; in June it is only 5.8°C. In general it is cool enough for permafrost to form, at least locally. I had often been told that it was absolutely safe to wade through the bogs in gum-boots: the hard surface of the permafrost, a foot below ground level, would serve to keep boots dry. Soon after my arrival, relying on this advice, I went boldly into a bog right up to my waist, filling both boots with mud. Afterwards I was more careful. Undeniably, however, in many places there was a smooth hard surface of evidently permanent ice a foot or so under the surface of the bog. I proved this by plunging my arm in and feeling the bottom.

Once in every decade, or even less often, the Varanger Peninsula experiences a real summer. I was fortunate, for 1972 was such a year. While England suffered wind and rain and unseasonably low temperatures through June and into July, Finnmark experienced a heat wave. On the Norwegian television weather map one evening North Norway was given 20°C while England had only 10°C. Already before the end of June it was said to be the hottest summer since 1960; by the time I left I was told it was the hottest summer for 100 years, even the hottest ever recorded. After a day or two of cool dull weather ending with a very wet and rainy morning on 14 June, things gradually improved. The weekend of 17–18 June was warm and sunny. Admittedly on 19 June, a 'fret' as it is called in Yorkshire, was coming in off the Barents Sea, swathing the eastern extremity of the peninsula in great banks of swirling white mist. But the next morning the weather on that wild and exposed north-east coast was brilliantly sunny and positively hot. Thereafter it was a question of one fine day after another. At Vadsø the municipal tulips put up a superb show of blossom in the third week of June. By the last week of the month the summer had acquired real distinction; an undeniable quality which was scarcely marred by occasional thunder clouds and showers (rather than real storms) early in July. Apart from a wet and cloudy afternoon on 3 July the fine hot weather continued nearly uninterrupted until 13

July, which was dry but overcast. So I left the peninsula on 15 July in brilliant sunshine, having experienced one of the most sustained and memorable spells of hot weather I have ever enjoyed in any country. Without this splendid weather the photographs in this book could never have been taken, and its title would be incomprehensible.

In common with the rest of North Norway the Varanger Peninsula experiences the midnight sun. At Vardø the sun is continuously above the horizon for 69 days, from 18 May to 26 July. The lighthouses in the Varanger Peninsula are closed down from 25 May until 11 August. The Norwegians appear to be able to adapt themselves so as to sleep but little through the summer and take advantage of the extra daylight. They apparently make up this sleep loss in the winter. I found it necessary to maintain my normal sleeping habits by turning in at around 2300 hours or midnight, and sleeping until 0700 or even 0730 hours. Sleep was not so sound as in darkness: I found that I awoke frequently though momentarily during the night. As the summer heat developed I was disconcerted to be woken up at 0300 hours not by the light of the sun, but by its heat, and I soon learnt that the effect of the midnight sun, in warm weather, was to produce stiflingly hot nights. The birds seem to have a quite definite rhythm of activity and inactivity. I watched a fieldfare start to roost on its nest around 1800 hours instead of continuing to feed its young, and most birds seemed to roost from about this time and to become active again from 0300 to 0400 hours.

During my five weeks in the Varanger Peninsula Vadsø was my base and headquarters. It was here that I bought petrol, obtained drinking water, collected mail, and purchased supplies of bread, milk and delicious Norwegian smoked salmon. It was here too that I brought my clothes to the laundry once a week and enjoyed a weekly bath. The Vadsø baths were a kind of informal club. There were two nights a week for women and two for men. Four crowns (17 kr=£1) bought a small piece of soap, a tiny towel, and up to two hours in a hot shower, a sauna, or swimming in a small heated pool twelve breast-strokes long. But the Vadsø baths offered more than that; they were a centre for the exchange of information and gossip. We sat on wooden benches in the nude and I had ample opportunity to practise my Norwegian, though there were always people there who spoke English. It was at the baths that I would discover the best route up some mountain or how high the temperature had risen that day; I even picked up information about birds. Vadsø also boasts an excellent library. I went there at the beginning of my stay and asked to have some books about local history and geography put out for me against a rainy day. But the rainy day never came in that glorious summer and

I only visited the library once more, to say an apologetic goodbye and collect a list of these books, which I subsequently borrowed through Inter-Library Loan at home. Another amenity of Vadsø which, because of the fine weather, I used only occasionally, was the Vadsø Hotel, where one could sit comfortably with drinks or coffee in the evening and write up one's journal and notes at a table.

Normally I slept in the car and, though it was possible to park and stop the night almost anywhere, I did tend to remain several nights in one place and to return again to a once-used site. Whenever I could find the time and the weather was suitable I developed films. I had brought processing equipment and chemicals for this, and had intended to develop two films every day. In the event, partly because of the fine weather, time did not allow this. It was not in any case an easy operation. The washing could be speeded up by using changes of sea water instead of fresh, but even then it was time-consuming. Drying was often a problem, especially in windy weather, or when there was no wind. Frequently it was difficult to keep the solutions sufficiently cool. In all, I only managed to develop about twenty of the 133 black and white films I exposed while I was still in the peninsula. The rest had to be processed at home after my return.

Although Vadsø was my base and my ornithological activities were concentrated in the coastal area between it and Krampenes, I made an effort to investigate other parts of the peninsula, many of which are described in the chapters which follow. Attention was paid to offshore islands: I spent two nights on the island of Vadsøya; single days on Hornøy off Vardø and on Lille Ekkerøy, and two days on Kongsøya off the north coast. I drove or was driven along virtually every road in the peninsula. I spent single nights at Berlevåg on the northern tip of the peninsula and at Sandfjord near Hamningberg in the north-east, and three nights in the interior near Hanglefjell. I explored the cliffs and birch woods of the Tomaselv valley, haunt of rough-legged buzzards in good lemming years, but quite devoid of these fine birds when I explored it. I investigated the birch woods and the open fells above Nesseby and Nyborg and the marshes near Varangerbotn. Kibymyr and the Langsmedvann near Vadsø were visited, and the Thirteen Lakes (Trettenvandene) above Krampenes. I had intended to abandon the car from time to time and take a light-weight tent, a hide and my cameras up into the hills, but in the event only two such expeditions were made, one to Syltefjordstauran on the north-east coast and the other to Sørfjell above Nesseby.

In all my wanderings in the Varanger Peninsula I was struck by the natural beauty of this wild and remote landscape, yet appalled by the ugliness and destruction wrought even here by man. The impact of his activities was certainly devastatingly apparent, nor were the Norwegians alone to blame. Litter was being dumped among roadside bushes or near unofficial camp-sites by visitors and tourists from several European countries. Broken glass was commonplace. In the wild interior of the peninsula I saw two boys throwing stones at bottles while their parents sat in a neighbouring caravan. Huts are everywhere, round every lake, along every river valley, even in that great expanse of marsh, Kibymyr, and often out in the open fell. It was difficult to photograph a landscape or a habitat without including one or more of these huts complete with their flagpoles and separate toilet huts. Moreover, telephone wires and power lines do not follow roads but take short cuts, marching, often for miles over the fells. Worst of all, perhaps, is the permanent and ugly scar left all along the new road between Krampenes and Svartnes. The stones have been scooped out in a wide swathe on either side by bulldozers, and heaped up to form the raised foundation for the road which must be essential to keep it open in the winter snows. The wonderful series of raised beaches above the present sea level, many of them untouched by vegetation other than pale grey-green lichens, others colonised over the centuries by a sparse growth of crowberry, have suffered permanent damage by being torn apart. The road is beautifully engineered for fast driving but not for scenic beauty, bordered as it now is by a wide expanse of bare rock and earth, incongruous and hideous in these wild and lovely surroundings. Communications have been improved, the landscape ruined. But perhaps it is not for me to complain. My own country has been plundered and mutilated by man on a far larger scale than Norway and, in spite of everything, the Varanger Peninsula is still profoundly and unmistakably dominated by the wild grandeur of unspoilt nature. It is noble country indeed.

Everywhere I went in the Varanger Peninsula people were kind and helpful in every possible way. In the pages which follow mention will be made of the two youthful ornithologists of Nesseby, Sverre and Willi, one of whom accompanied me to Sørfjell in search of dotterels, and of Aage Olsen and Terje Daldorff who took me to Kongsøya. Subsequently Terje and his wife entertained me to coffee, pastries and cloudberry jam in their house at Berlevåg. At 2300 hours they drove me to Molvik and thereafter we walked along the most northerly beach in the Varanger Peninsula to its north-west extremity, a mighty cliff called the Tanahorn. It was a Norwegian's evening stroll: a mere five miles there and another five back, accomplished after midnight. At first we walked along a wide, flat, crowberry-covered raised beach with towering cliffs on our left and the brilliant midnight sun shining over the Barents Sea on our right. Then we picked our way over rocks, Terje showed me a sea-eagle's eyrie, sadly deserted since 1970. Returning, we scoured the beach for those decorative glass fishing floats which are now no longer made. It was piled high in places with massive timbers from Russia, for no timber of any kind grows on the northern coasts of Norway. We found a Russian tin and several English tobacco tins, and Terje showed me an ancient whale jaw-bone, half buried in the shingle. When we arrived back at his home at 0200 hours he asked me in to coffee! Like Aage Olsen, Terje Daldorff did not speak English. This was one reaon why these two meant much to me: with them I could attempt to speak Norwegian.

Among other Norwegians I met was Leon Johansson of Vadsø, who was extremely kind and helpful and, like so many of his countrymen, an enthusiast for things English. One of the saddest moments of my whole visit to Norway was when I had to refuse his invitation to spend an evening with him in his family's very pleasant modern house on the outskirts of Vadsø: I just could not find a spare moment. He is an active and enthusiastic ornithologist who gave me a great deal of useful information. Twice while at Vadsø I had the good fortune to meet and talk at his home with Erling Sundve, who divided his time in summer between his two grocer's shops, one in Vadsø and the other at Hamningberg. Somehow he finds time to photograph birds, write about them in the local paper, and take parties of ornithologists from Norway, Germany, Sweden and elsewhere in his boat across the waters of the Syltefjord to visit the world's most northerly gannet colony at Syltefjordstauran. He too was a mine of ornithological information. He showed me a book he had written and illustrated and printed privately on the Coto Doñana in the south of Spain, the opposite corner of Europe to his own.

Then of course there were bird-watchers from other European countries besides Norway at work in the Varanger Peninsula. I came across several English parties and individuals, who came and went for brief periods. There were Swedes too. I met a French couple who spoke enthusiastically about the birds they had seen and the nests they had found, and several Germans, including a couple from Stuttgart who showed me a roadside shorelark's nest, the young just fledging, on 19 June. They told me of the ground-nesting fieldfares at Sandfjord, where no trees grew. A Dutch couple, Hidde and Lucie Bult, who unfortunately left not long after I arrived, were also extremely helpful to me. He is from Frisia, and was studying biochemistry at the University of Utrecht. Without his aid I should probably never have photographed the bluethroat: he showed me a nest containing seven eggs. I was fortunate in that the language of this international ornithological fraternity was English. Many of them were amassing valuable data about the birds of the Varanger Peninsula and one hopes that these records will be published or, perhaps better, sent to Jostein Grastveit of Vadsø.

More than a word or two needs to be said here about Jostein Grastveit, for in him I found a kindred spirit and fellow enthusiast, an informant, an adviser, a helper, a host and, above all, a friend. The success of my expedition to the Varanger Peninsula was due, as I afterwards realised, to two things: the weather and Jostein Grastveit.

Brought up on his father's farm in South Norway, Jostein Grastveit, then a thirty-four-year-old bachelor with short-cropped very blond hair, is an open-air enthusiast who does his utmost to counteract the enervating effects of his office job by a cult of physical exercise. One evening I paced him in the car as, after a bird-watching expedition along the coast, he cycled furiously downhill into Vadsø in a blue track-suit. I won't say that I found it hard to keep up with him, but at one point I did think we would exceed the speed limit. His hours of work, a sensible 0830 to 1530 hours, allow him time to get out in the evenings, at least in summer. He came to Finnmark of his own volition about five years ago and took a job with the local power company, the Varanger Kraftlag. Although this has occasionally provided him with opportunities for camping trips in various parts of the Varanger Peninsula to inspect power lines and so on, it also means that, during one week in five, he has to take his turn on telephone duty staying at home every evening and throughout the weekend ready to deal with complaints and emergencies.

Jostein's ornithological activities are characterised by their passionate dedication and extraordinary diversity. They benefit from his superb physical condition. Who else but a supremely physically fit person like Jostein would have dared to launch an investigation into the birds of Kibymyr and conduct it nearly single-handed, striding time after time into the very heart of that formidable five-mile-long morass whose outer fringes are sufficient to deter most people from further investigation? But, not content with this, he and some friends have organised and obtained finance for co-operative enquiries into the birds of several other key localities round the shores of the Varanger Fjord. But Jostein is a ringer too. Between 1914 and 1966 some 100 red-necked phalaropes were ringed in Norway. Since then, Jostein himself has personally ringed over 1,000, trapping them in mist-nets over the pools they frequent along the southern shore of the peninsula. At least three weeks of his annual four-week holiday have lately been spent living in a tent by the phalarope pool on Vadsøya, almost within sight of his flat in Vadsø, ringing phalaropes. Besides all this, Jostein is a keen and expert bird photographer, with an artistic eye. He had equipped himself with a motor-driven Nikon and a 640 mm Novoflex lens and has achieved the distinction of a colour picture on the cover of the Norwegian ornithological journal *Sterna* and a beautifully illustrated article, the subject of both of which was Steller's eiders in Vadsø harbour. Indeed, Jostein has made himself a considerable expert on eiders: after all, at times in the spring he can see a flock of 2,000 king eiders swimming in the fjord below his office window. This was the man who entertained me in his flat, accompanied me to Kongsfjord and Syltefjord, and assisted me in every possible way. I was not by any means the first foreign visitor who has been helped and encouraged by this charming and enthusiastic man; nor will I be the last.

Jostein Grastveit on the fells above Golnes.

Opposite, top: *The capital of Finnmark County, Vadsø, on the southern shore of the Varanger Peninsula, dominated by its modern church and twin radio masts. Behind and above the town is the lonely and partly snow-covered fell.*

The Arctic Ocean Highway is the only road which crosses the interior of the peninsula. Built in 1959, it is closed by snow during the winter months. Opposite, bottom: *looking westwards towards Leirpollen.* Below: *looking north over Kongsfjord Fell. 16 June 1972.*

Opposite: *The fish drying racks at Kongsfjord, on the north coast of the Varanger Peninsula. Here and elsewhere fieldfares nest on these racks (see above), far beyond the limit of trees.*

Above: *A fieldfare's nest with six eggs on the fish-drying racks at Kongsfjord photographed on 18 June. The nest and eggs are closely similar to those of the blackbird, which however is unknown in the Varanger Peninsula.*

Although much of the Varanger Peninsula has no vegetation whatsoever, a single species of tree, the birch, is found in parts of the west and south. One of the best developed and most extensive birch forests in the peninsula, seen above, is in the valley of the Julelv.

Well beyond the tree line on the peninsula's north-east coast, a thriving fieldfare colony nests here at Sandfjord on the rocks and even on the ground. Typically, a wooden hut has been set up in the wilderness for summer use. Above it may be seen some of the splendid raised beaches which are found all round the shores of north Norway.

Kongsøya and Syltefjordstauran

3

Even though they are both ornithologically well known, I could not forbear to visit the two most important sea-bird colonies on the rugged north-east coast of the Varanger Peninsula. Kongsøya is an island in Kongsfjord, which faces north-eastwards towards the Barents Sea. Syltefjordstauran is, literally, the stack of Syltefjord; it harbours a section only of the large sea-bird colony scattered along the southern cliffs of the headland known as Syltefjordklubben. The Syltefjord too faces north-east. Kongsøya, the king's island, was visited 16-18 June and Syltefjordstauran on 24-25 June. The birds of the two are dissimilar: Kongsøya is dominated by cormorants and shags, black guillemots, herring and greater black-backed gulls and eiders; Syltefjordstauran by gannets, guillemots, and kittiwakes. Kongsøya has low, slightly developed cliffs; Syltefjordstauran is backed by a 400 feet precipice.

My visit to Kongsøya was due to Jostein, and it was he who made the necessary arrangements with the owner of the island, Aage Olsen of Veines, for us to be taken over by boat and to have the use of the stoutly-built and well-appointed wooden hut on the island. A drive of several hours is needed to reach Veines from Vadsø, and I had time for only one stop on the way, by the mouth of the River Tana. Here, while cooking my 'mid-day' meal at about 1430 hours on 16 June I disturbed an elegant greenshank from a roadside pool; it flew off up into the fells where it doubtless had a nest. It was the only one I saw in the Varanger Peninsula. It was a calm, cool, more or less cloudy day as I admired the scene around me. Northwards I was looking across the vast Tana sand flats at the three-quarters snow-capped peak of the highest mountain in the Varanger Peninsula. Below the snowy summit the rounded grey-buff rock slopes descended to the flat river mouth. All round me was flat sand with pools of water but, southwards, the sand on both sides of the road was grass-grown; Temmincks's stints were trilling loudly over it; and there were patches of crowberry. Further away the grass gave way to birch scrub, still growing on absolutely flat ground. Beyond the scrub was a remarkable series of embattlemented precipices extending for several kilometres above the Tana River valley and the road along which I had come. Westwards the view extented across the Tana to range after range of snowy fells; eastwards the Varanger Peninsula itself was partly in view. Already the birch was bursting into leaf and the sepia-coloured lower slopes of a week ago were now green – a transformation which seemed to have come about almost overnight.

After the Tana mouth the road climbs up through the birch forest and over the bare stony fells of the interior, past some of the most beautiful scenery I have ever seen. There was snow everywhere; the

The bluethroat is one of the most colourful of Arctic passerines; it virtually posed near its nest for me to photograph it.

Whimbrel at nest. This bird's eggs were already chipped when this photograph was taken on 29 June.

Incubating turnstone. This is one of the most attractive and characteristic breeding waders of the Varanger Peninsula.

road was bordered by snow cliffs, several metres high in places where the snow ploughs had only recently cut their way through the drifts. Along the still mostly snow-covered shores of a large lake, I stopped briefly to look at the birds. A ringed plover was displaying, performing its low, weaving 'butterfly-winged' flight over the melting ice of the lake. A snipe was chipping and drumming, Temminck's stints were trilling; and a bluethroat was in full song.

At Veines, Aage Olsen and his wife, though they themselves could not be present, had laid out a sumptuous tea for us. Soon afterwards we were splashing across the waters of Kongsfjord in Aage Olsen's boat, with Terje Daldorff at the helm. As we drew nearer Kongsøya I felt the ever-recurrent excitement of a visit to a sea-bird island, heightened on this occasion by the fact that it was uninhabited and that Jostein and I were to live there for two days on our own. Kongsøya is a great green and grey hump standing out of Kongsfjord. Around it the ice-cold blue waters of the Barents Sea are backed on three sides by a wild, deserted, rocky shore, virtually devoid of vegetation. In contrast to this surrounding mainland rock desert, Kongsøya supports an extraordinarily rich vegetation: it is a botanist's paradise. Grass grows here luxuriantly, ferns too, and the cloudberry occupies large areas. A superb patch of marsh marigolds were in full bloom while we were there; and much of the island was covered by a sweet-scented white crucifer. Three weeks later the entire island looked pink through binoculars from the mainland; apparently it was swathed in a dense growth of rosebay willow herb. I wished I had had time to look at this extraordinary plant life. After a quick walk round the island immediately after our arrival, Jostein and I installed ourselves in the wooden hut, and Jostein lit the stove with some of the neatly chopped driftwood stacked ready for use. He had collected three herring gull's eggs from nests containing one egg only and laughed at the six brown hen's eggs I had brought from England. Unfortunately, however, none of the gull's eggs proved fresh enough to be edible. We turned in, in our sleeping bags on the roughly-made wooden bunks and listened to the creaking of the hut as a freshening breeze from the south came in over the fjord.

SATURDAY 17 JUNE 1972. Jostein and I spent the entire day clambering about on Kongsøya photographing birds. At 0630 hours when we got up it was sunny but cool and windy. By 1300 hours, when without a shirt I sat on a rock by the hut to eat my lunch, the sun was bright and hot, the wind had subsided to a breeze, and the sky was mostly blue. It was balmy, warm and altogether lovely on that splendid island. The most conspicuous birds were several thousand pairs of herring gulls and over 100 pairs of great black-backed gulls. These birds' nests were scattered all over the grassy slopes between the rocky ridges which run more or less parallel along the length of the island. Only a few young were found, but most of the first clutches had been taken by commercial eggers. When I paused for a cup of tea at 1630 hours, sitting on a log outside the hut, the only sound was the calls of these gulls and the only birds visible were the gulls, which could be seen on the slopes and rocks above, some incubating, some standing near their nests. The sea was absolutely still and calm; the sky serene.

An accurate count of all Kongsøya's breeding birds would be a major undertaking. There must be at least fifty pairs of eiders, and probably over 100. Wherever you walk, the ducks suddenly explode out of the ground, usually fouling the nest with a yellowish evil-smelling dropping, perhaps designed to deter predators from eating the eggs. Most clutches are of three or four eggs, half buried in the soft grey down. But, if you happen to see it in time, you can often walk past near the nest without disturbing the sitting bird. One exceptionally confiding duck allowed me to photograph her at a range of one metre with the standard lens of my Nikon.

Kongsøya is rightly famed for its breeding cormorants: over 100 pairs nest in scattered groups along the cliffs, and two dozen or more pairs of shags nest near them though somewhat apart. I put up a hide on the cliff top near one group of nesting cormorants so that I could watch and photograph these birds behaving normally, instead of in a perpetual state of alarm at the human presence near their nests. All save one pair had chicks, varying in development from tiny naked things still being brooded by their parents, to large well-feathered juveniles. Jostein, who ringed a number, saw one juvenile actually flying. The adult cormorants have a pleasing, sonorous croak; the young ones beg plaintively for food with a repeated 'per-wheep', 'per-wheep', at the same time vibrating their heads and wings. A few herring gulls were nesting here with the cormorants. Every time one of these gulls approached too near a cormorant's nest with two large young, the young and old cormorants cawed loudly in unison and lunged their heads and necks towards the intruder. From my hide I could watch two shags' nests and ten cormorants'; and I could admire, too, the beautiful blue-green eyes of both species.

The exact number of black guillemots breeding among the boulder slopes of Kongsøya, especially on the western side of the island, would be hard to establish with certainty: fifty pairs, perhaps. These dumpy black and white birds with their bright pink feet zoom out from under the boulders, as one clambers along the slope below the cliffs, and then sit about, squatting on their bellies, on the rocks. Their courtship is charming: two birds sit facing each other, uttering a curious high pitched whispering note, while bowing their heads at one another and touching their beaks together.

Auks on Kongsøya are few and far between: I saw only up to 10 puffins together, and even fewer razorbills. Nor are kittiwakes particularly numerous, being confined to the cliffs at the island's northern end, where there are some dense concentrations, and to a low sea-smoothed rock near the hut, where the nests are at shoulder height above the beach and very easily accessible. It was the first time I had ever been able to touch and examine kittiwakes' nests at close quarters. Apart from two flattened pads of material which could not properly be described as nests, all the ten nests in this little colony contained eggs – six 2-egg clutches and three single-egg clutches; none of three eggs. The nests seemed identical to those I am familiar with in Yorkshire, though viewed there through binoculars. Constructed of grass roots and grass and lumps of turf, feathers and seaweed, they were very damp inside and matted with droppings outside, which showed the usual delicate turquoise stains. What made this unusual kittiwake colony still more unusual was the presence of breeding common gulls. There were about 4-6 pairs of these birds, and two of the nests were on the rounded top of the kittiwakes' rock, one of them only three feet from the nearest kittiwakes' nest. Other common gulls' nests were on the neighbouring shingle beach. Aage Olsen told me that kittiwakes have spread considerably. A few years ago they were confined to the northern tip of the island and there were only a few pairs there. Now, there may be 1,000 pairs in all. To complete the tally of Kongsøya's breeding birds, the oystercatchers must be mentioned. The first of a clutch of three eggs on the beach near the hut hatched in the night of 17-18 June. There were, too, about three pairs of rock pipits, one of which was feeding young, and a pair of hooded crows. The willow wren, white wagtail and redpolls also present may not have been breeding.

At midday on Sunday 18 June Aage Olsen came to ferry us back to the mainland. This remarkable man might be described as the principal inhabitant of Veines, if one could be sure that there were any others. As a matter of fact there are a few other houses besides his own in this remote and minute outpost of humanity. Aage owns or rents seven different islands, three of them in Kongsfjord and four round the next headland to the west. What on earth for? Well, Aage is a connoisseur and lover of islands. He has built himself huts on some of them so that he can stay there. But Kongsøya at least is also a profit-making concern. In return for an annual rent, paid to the Norwegian government, of 750 crowns,he takes and sells two important crops: the eggs of the herring gulls, up to 25,000 in a good year, and the cloudberries which grow profusely on the island. In May-June he can hope to receive some 3,000 crowns for the gulls' eggs, and in August up to 9,000 crowns for cloudberries. But Aage is no capitalist in spite of these land-owning and money-making pretensions. He is a short, cheerful, humorous middle-aged Norwegian – indeed a thoroughly entertaining person. Out of the locker of his boat he produced the most extraordinary piece of headgear I have ever seen: a battered old black leather, part furred, peaked cap. This he claimed to have found on the beach: it was a Russian officer's hat. He later produced a second hat, a soft dome-shaped felt cap with a small peak: this was the hat of an English lord! When we arrived at Veines, Mrs Olsen, who whiles away the long winter weaving superb tapestries on a hand loom, had prepared a meal for us of thick soup, cake and coffee. Aage showed us his armoury. First he produced a gun which he jokingly told us he had used to shoot the Russian officer; then he put it away and brought out a larger gun. Finally he came out with a huge rifle equipped with telescopic sights, which looked as if it could make short work of a Polar bear. We drove back to Vadsø in brilliant warm sunshine which everywhere sparkled on melting snow. Floes of thick glassy ice floated down the rivers and water spouted out of the base of every snowdrift. Summer had arrived.

A week later, on Friday 23 June, Jostein and I drove off from Vadsø bound this time for Syltefjord. We camped the night on the shores of the fjord by one of the tiny settlements round its head. Everywhere people were lighting their midsummer bonfires; it was the eve of Sankt Hans. Snowdrifts extended here virtually to sea level, but there were patches of willow scrub along the river valleys and scattered hayfields by the fjord, as well as much bare lichen-covered ground. It could not conceivably have been a finer midsummer night: the air was calm, warm and still. Redwings and bramblings were singing away; evidently there was enough scrub for these species to nest even here. Common gulls were breeding in and near the villages; fieldfares' and hooded crows' nests were seen on the fish-drying racks. A skylark was singing away above our heads, and we repeatedly heard curlews calling: these two species have spread during the last thirty or fifty years through the Varanger Peninsula as far as there are hayfields for them to nest in.

Next morning we set out from the hamlet of Syltefjord, heavily laden with photographic and camping equipment, to walk along the rugged northern shore of the fjord to the famous stack where the world's most northern gannetry was discovered in 1961, then two pairs strong. Although breeding seabirds are concentrated along a three kilometre stretch of cliffs over 100 m high, our lack of a boat on this occasion and the brief time available meant that we could hope to do little more than see the Syltefjordstaur with its breeding gannets. The walk was by no means easy. Route-finding was difficult and in any event a very steep rocky slope had to be negotiated. Nor could we avoid crossing a river which looked like a stream until we actually tried to wade through it. The water was freezing cold, the boulders which formed the bottom extremely slippery, the current was strong, and we had to remove our boots and trousers because the water was up to our thighs in places. Even the giant Jostein, used to this sort of thing, found it difficult going; for me it would have been quite impossible without his help. Indeed he carried my rucksack over for me. Once safely past this hazard, we were faced with a weary climb over a surface of jagged, jumbled boulders. In places brilliant yellow-green lichens grew on these stones; elsewhere they were utterly devoid of even this primitive vegetation. As one walked over these boulders they moved and clanked against each other and one could even detect a smell of burning from this friction in that still warm air. Jostein, more surefooted than I, led the way and I followed, his enormous rucksack, with bedroll, water bottle and other paraphernalia dangling from it, seeming to tower above my head. While this extraordinary man balanced, leaped and picked his way through the boulder jungle, he held a Nikon attached to a 400 mm Novoflex lens in his free hand!

The landscape we traversed was wild, utterly lonely, and magnificent. The fjord on our right was backed by gaunt barren mountains, flecked with snow. After a trudge along the shore we ascended to the brow of a rocky ridge, our way barred by a precipice. It was here that we were lucky enough to stumble on some newly-fledged young ravens. The first we startled and it flew off at once; the second was loath to go. It had perhaps never flown before. In any case it was unwilling to launch out over the precipice and instead sat on the edge, eyeing us suspiciously, even allowing us to approach near enough for photography. Far below us a vast stony plain backed the fjord coastline, here curved into a bay. Behind this coastline, and parallel to it and to each other, was a splendid series of raised beaches, all gently curving. Close inspection showed that they were formed of large rounded boulders, now encrusted with lichen. In this plain a pair of long-tailed ducks obligingly settled on a pool not far from us, and our march was again interrupted while we photographed these lovely birds as they swam on the pool and then stood on the bank side by side. Near the stream we found a dense pack of kittiwakes resting on the shore and bathing in the fresh water at the stream mouth. These, too, we could not resist stopping to photograph. As we approached along the sand, a great thickly-packed mass of these birds flew up and away, but still huge numbers remained on the beach, departing in several successive waves over the sea as we drew nearer.

In the early afternoon we arrived at last on the stony cliff top directly above the Syltefjordstaur. Here some flat peaty ground in a shallow depression, partly covered by a large snowdrift, formed a welcome contrast to the jumbled boulders we had walked across. We pitched our tents here on the grass and clambered down a steep scree slope to find a place on the rocks perhaps 20 m above the sea, whence one could see well the famous gannets breeding on the stack. Without a boat it was hard to ascertain the total number, but 27 nests appeared to be visible from this side, and about 54-6 adult birds. A good many of the nests contained a quite large white downy chick with a black face, in size somewhat larger than the neighbouring guillemots. The gannets all seemed to be at about the same stage; none was seen to be incubating and only one chick seemed to be substantially larger than the others. They occupied parts of the top of the stack; further down were some thick concentrations of guillemots and kittiwakes, the latter mostly still incubating eggs, though a few had small young. The only other birds seen to be nesting on the stack itself were three or four pairs of herring gulls, one with quite well grown chicks. Although next morning I explored a mile or more of cliff top north-eastwards while Jostein photographed his beloved gannets, I only managed to see a small section of what is in fact Norway's largest kittiwake colony. The Norwegian sea-bird expert, Einar Brun, reckoned there were a quarter million pairs here in 1967 and, in 1969, he recorded 12,300 pairs of guillemots and about 1,200 pairs of razorbills. Herring gulls seemed to me to be few and far between, and the only greater black-backed gulls we saw were at the foot of the cliffs, apparently not breeding. The honk of ravens was audible the whole time we were in the area, but I could not ascertain whether these birds, or *Larus* gulls, or some other predator (? foxes), was responsible for the large numbers of sucked kittiwakes', and a few other, eggs, which were lying about all over the boulder slopes above the cliffs.

Although we saw the odd pied wagtail, meadow pipit and wheatear on our way to Syltefjordstauran, these species were not present at our camp site some 150 m above the sea. Instead, redpolls flew over several times singing, or perched on the rocks, two bramblings flew past, and three Arctic skuas sailed high overhead, calling. At night, from the tents, we heard the sweet jingling song of the snow bunting and the ptarmigan's extraordinary call, like an incredibly squeaky door swinging to and fro. The snow bunting was quite common here. I came across several as I clambered over the giant stone-fields on the Sunday morning, picking my way over jagged, reddish, often sharp-edged boulders, many with brilliant yellow-green patches of lichen on them. It was a sizzling hot day: a few small white clouds floated in a blue sky; the snow-drifts were blindingly white. On the march back, into a scorching sun, it was excruciatingly hot as we toiled across the stones, over the raised beaches, and finally along the rocky present day beach. We made lemon squash with the ice-cold water of a mountain stream when we got back to the car and picnicked by the road during our four hour drive home to Vadsø in the soft evening light.

An eider duck incubating in a typical Kongsøya nest-site: a well-sheltered hollow in a grassy bank. This bird, untypically, allowed close approach.

Above: *The views from Kongsøya's western slopes, looking southwards across to the mainland Varanger Peninsula. Cormorants and herring gulls are the two commonest breeding sea-birds on Kongsøya. Here, they are nesting in close proximity.*

The black guillemot (opposite) *breeds in some numbers on Kongsøya among the jumbled boulders at the foot of the cliffs.* Top: *a pair of black guillemots courting: both birds make a curious high-pitched whispering note, while the wings are slightly outspread and the tail cocked up.*

Opposite, top: *Young and old cormorants shriek and posture with open gapes and lunging heads at a herring gull which flies past too close to their nests.* Above: *A cormorant family on Kongsøya: an adult with two well-grown young.*

Opposite, bottom: *Close-up of the head of an incubating shag on Kongsøya. This bird was most unwilling to leave its nest. The shags were somewhat behind the cormorants in their breeding schedule. The nests I examined on 17 June contained either eggs or small naked young.*

A raven's first flight? We surprised this newly-fledged young raven on our way to Syltefjordstauran. For a long time it perched about on the cliff edge (opposite), *reluctant to take wing. At last* (above), *it took the plunge and sailed majestically away. The raven is a characteristic Syltefjord bird.*

Overleaf: *Kittiwakes near Syltefjord: part of a large gathering on the beach by the mouth of a stream which flows into the fjord; they had assembled to bathe in and drink the fresh water.*

Above: *Two non-breeding members of Syltefjordstauran's gannet colony. The bird scratching its head is standing on a rudimentary nest.*

Opposite: *The stack of Syltefjord with part of the rugged northern shore of the fjord showing behind it.*

Eiders and other ducks

4

Of all the birds of the Varanger Peninsula the common eider is one of the most numerous and characteristic. It is found all round the coast, and may often be seen, too, on the lakes inland. On 26 June I saw a party of fourteen ducks and a single drake on a lake behind Golnes; instead of making their usual restrained 'who-hoo' note, these birds were quacking loudly. Typically, at any rate early in the season, the eider flocks are predominantly of males; at the head of Syltefjord on 23 June almost all of the 150 birds present were males. On the other hand on 6 July some 30 eider ducks were swimming together off the island of Lille Ekkerøy with no males in sight.

Although the eider breeds all along the mainland shore of the Varanger Peninsula, it is on offshore islands that it forms relatively dense breeding concentrations or colonies. Presumably these are secure from the depredations of foxes and possibly other predators. Kongsøya was such a one. Another eider colony was on the island of Lille Ekkerøy, which I visited on 6 July. Few drakes were to be seen; by this late date they would be moulting into the so-called eclipse plumage, the first sign of which I had seen on 28 June. But the ducks were everywhere, flying off heavily and low as you disturbed groups of ten or fifteen of them standing about on the island slopes. Besides these birds, apparently without nests, others would suddenly shamble off their two, three, or four eggs, literally from under your feet, and then fly. The nests were in all kinds of situations; on grassy cliff ledges, in flat grassy areas right out in the open, in a natural hollow, or sheltered by a bank or boulder. Only a few broods of ducklings could be seen on the sea: my very first eider ducklings had only been seen the day before, 5 July, in the tiny harbour at Krampenes on the mainland immediately opposite.

Although the drake eiders of the Varanger Peninsula were by no means tame, they could be watched and photographed on the shore in certain places from a hide or even from a car. The best place for them was the peninsula of Store Ekkerøy, which was an island until during the early part of the nineteenth century, it became connected to the mainland by a sand bar which is now more than 100 yards wide. A car can be driven along a large part of the north shore of Store Ekkerøy where low stony beach is much favoured by eiders. This was a favourite camp-site of mine, for there was a splendid view over the grey-blue waters of the fjord to the smooth flattish uplands of the mainland Varanger Peninsula with the huge flat snow-covered dome of Falkefjell rising in the centre. On 11 June I parked the car near this beach, and awoke next morning at 0400 hours to find that the tide had risen and brought the feeding eiders close to the car. I was able to watch and photograph them from a half-opened window, with the car's curtains still drawn. Some were in pairs, feeding in masses of floating seaweed. Sometimes the drake sat looking on while the duck fed eagerly. The characteristic 'ou-ooh', 'oo-who' notes could be heard from time to time. One duck lunged at another; a drake threw back his head rhythmically. Two duck eiders on the water chased one another with much splashing; later two ducks were scrapping. All this in the calm still early morning of 12 June. While the eiders fed on decaying seaweed and then rested on a group of boulders nearby other birds fed along the shore near the car: phalaropes bobbed up and down on the sea; bar-tailed godwits and purple sandpipers picked their way among the rocks; dunlins trilled and flew after one another.

On 13 June I installed myself in the hide at 0400 hours. It had been set up the day before overlooking some rock slabs, near the little harbour of Ekkerøy on which I had noticed eiders gathering at high tide. The common eiders, which soon returned to the rocks whence I had disturbed them in getting into the hide, were joined by a pair of Steller's eiders. This bird is much smaller than the eider. Both sexes have a curious black belly and bills which are different from the eider's, but their head-throwing display is similar. The common eiders were silent most of the time, but occasionally a drake would call 'oo-who-oo' and throw his head up; while the ducks uttered from time to time a gobbling, quacky call like a farm-yard duck. Soon after 0500 hours eiders were approaching to within 11-15 m of the hide, encouraged by a still-rising tide. The drake eider is an astonishingly lovely bird in its brilliant black and white breeding plumage, but the duck, when seen at close quarters, is very lovely too, with her very finely-barred breast, more broadly barred black and buff back, and an admixture of warm brownish feathers on back and wings. After a most successful session, I packed up at 0735 hours. It was a calm, peaceful sunny morning; the waters of the Varanger Fjord were tinted a lovely pale blue and, as always, were crystal clear.

Steller's eider is one of the ornithological specialities of the Varanger Peninsula. Although there is at least one record of apparent breeding, it seems clear that this little duck does not normally breed in Norway, nor indeed probably anywhere west of the delta of the River Lena in eastern Siberia. Flocks of up to 100 or more have, however, frequented the northern shores of the Varanger Fjord in summer ever since Blair recorded them, and searched in vain for nests, in the 1930s. But these birds are present in the winter, too, along the unfrozen north Norwegian coast, and in the Varanger Fjord. Their numbers increase rapidly in the spring, and Jostein Grastveit has recorded over 1,000 along the northern shore of the fjord in recent years in March, and flocks several hundred strong occur in Vadsø harbour at that time of year.

The Steller's eider drake is a most attractive little bird with curious colour similarities to the drake common eider. Both birds are predominantly white, but both have conspicuous black areas of plumage too, though in different places, and both have a pale green patch on the back of the head. Steller's eider has a rather odd-looking round black spot on the side of its breast, which does not look nearly so rufous as some bird books would have us believe. When I camped by the wooden church at Nesseby at the beginning of July there were 100 or more Steller's eiders swimming in the fjord and feeding along the shore. As is usual with the summer flocks of these birds in this area, nearly all were drakes; indeed at Nesseby the main flock was entirely of drakes, though a single duck was seen nearby. These drake Steller's eiders were beginning to look scruffy and streaky by 1 July: their annual moult had begun. On 6 July the seventy-strong flock at Lille Ekkerøy, nearly all drakes, looked very mottled. These birds feed in shallow water especially at low tide, swimming along with their heads under water and up-ending in the tidal pools, keeping in tight packs. Obviously, feeding is a highly sociable and co-operative operation in these circumstances. They also feed by diving, and I found the birds at Nesseby almost impossible to count. They swam about in such tight squadrons that it was hard to distinguish individual birds. When one did start counting such a flock, one or two would invariably dive, others would follow, until in a moment only two or three birds were left on the surface. Counting had to start all over again!

The king eider is far from being a rare bird on the Varanger coasts and a few are probably present during most summers, though the species has not yet been proved to breed. Again, numbers reach a peak in the spring. Jostein Grastveit (1971) has successfully photographed them in Vadsø harbour where they congregate at that time of year with the common and Steller's eiders. He made it clear that the concentrations of eiders in the Varanger Fjord in spring were associated with the movement of capelin into the fjord at that time of year. More recently Gjosaeter and others (1972) have published an interesting observation of a flock of c. 1,300 ducks which were proved to be feeding on capelin eggs at a spawning ground off the north-east coast of the Varanger Peninsula not far north of Vardø. About three-quarters of these birds were king eiders; the remainder were common eiders and long-tailed ducks. They were taking capelin eggs off the bottom between 25 and 30 m below the surface, between 30 March and 19 April 1972.

After the eiders, perhaps the most characteristic and attractive of the Varanger Peninsula's breeding ducks are the goosander and long-tailed duck. Both species are common. Drake goosanders can be seen almost anywhere along the shore in the early summer; long-tailed ducks frequent the lakes, inland but also coastal pools. Photography of these birds is by no means easy. I spent hours in a hide by the mouth of the River Storelv after I disturbed a flock of goosanders there on one occasion. But the birds never returned while I was there, and all I managed to obtain was a very distant photograph of two of them, one of which was pointing its head and bill skywards in the typical display posture. Time and again I saw goosanders feeding close inshore and tried to stalk them. But the wary ducks, always the first in a mixed flock to take alarm and go, never gave me even a distant opportunity. Needless to say, I never found a nest of either of these species; nor indeed of any other species of duck apart from eiders, though I saw teal, pintail, widgeon, scaup, tufted duck, common scoter and numerous goldeneyes and red-breasted mergansers. It seems possible that the numbers of breeding ducks have declined in recent years. As to divers, these were decidedly sparse; I personally saw an occasional red-throated diver but not a single black-throated, though my Dutch friend Hidde Bult recorded one.

A flotilla of eider ducks swims round the rocky southern shore of Lille Ekkerøy. Many pairs were nesting on this island.

Above: *Store Ekkerøy. A rare sight indeed: people sunbathe and swim in the waters of the Varanger Fjord in the unusually hot summer of 1972.*

Opposite: *A pair of common eiders resting at high tide.*

Below: *Common eider at Store Ekkerøy, photographed on the shore at high tide from a hide. Swimming close inshore, the duck shows itself to be by no means the dull brown bird it so often seems from a distance.*

Bottom: *A handsome black-and-white drake long-tailed duck rises from the edge of a pool near the main road beyond Store Ekkerøy.*

Looking west from the cliffs of Store Ekkerøy's southern shore, 5 July. To the left of the wooden houses behind the harbour are fenced-in hayfields and, on the extreme left, the fish-drying racks so characteristic of north Norwegian fishing villages. In the foreground, sheep are grazing in an enclosure near some carefully cultivated vegetable plots. A pair of shorelarks nested in the grass by the two round concrete structures in the middle distance – remains of war-time German gun emplacements. The author's motor caravan is parked just beyond the vegetable plots. Wheatears were feeding young in a hole in the cliffs near at hand.

A drake Steller's eider swimming. The black spots round the eye and on the side of the breast are distinctive features of this bird's attractive plumage.

Four drake Steller's eiders on a rock at high tide. Top: *the right hand bird lunges aggressively at its neighbour with wings partly raised.* Bottom: *the neighbour takes to flight.*

Gulls, terns and skuas

5

Like other sea birds, the gulls, terns and skuas are well represented in the Varanger Peninsula, though it is too far north for some common species to breed regularly; for example the common tern and black-headed gull are virtually absent. Four species of gull nest in numbers: the greater black-backed, herring gull, common gull and kittiwake; there are two species of skua breeding, the Arctic and long-tailed; but of terns, only one occurs, the Arctic tern.

The black-headed gull, which has been extending its range northwards in Norway since it began breeding in the south in 1880, is still rather uncommon in the Varanger Peninsula, but a pair nested in 1967 on an island in the fjord. I saw one at Nesseby on 23 June and 2 July, and two at Ekkerøy on 10 June; in the summer of 1963 about fourteen spent two weeks near Vardø (Haftorn, 1971).

Another gull which occurs, but without breeding, is the glaucous gull, a bird which does, however, breed not far away, along the Murman coast of Russia. Although odd glaucous gulls occur here and there in summer all round the coast of the Varanger Peninsula, they are perhaps most often seen at Berlevåg, where abundant fish waste sustains numbers of gulls throughout the year, and it was there that I located two or three individuals among thousands of herring and greater black-backed gulls, on 10 and 11 July. It was smelly and difficult work picking one's way past heaps of fish-heads along the slippery quays, trying to single out a brown but white wing-tipped juvenile glaucous gull among so many other gulls wheeling round and round over the harbour in endless noisy circles.

In spite of a scatter of nests round the coasts and, of the common gull, inland, most of the Varanger Peninsula's gulls are concentrated in the breeding season on offshore islands like Kongsøya, where there are no foxes. The largest colonies of *Larus* gulls are probably those on Hornøy and Reinøy and nearby islets, off Vardø, whence large numbers of herring gulls' eggs are taken annually for human consumption. Older authors, Trevor-Battye for example, writing in 1895, reported lesser black-backed gulls breeding off Vardø, but, though its range extends up the west coast of Norway as far north as the latitude of Vardø, it has apparently never nested in the Varanger Peninsula. Trevor-Battye must have confused it with the great black-backed gull, which is widespread. I watched some of these birds on Hornøy; one of them was eagerly devouring a kittiwake. They eat the bodies but leave the wings, and there were dozens of these mangled kittiwake wings, often still attached in pairs, lying about near the breeding cliffs.

Another interesting off-shore islet, which I visited on 6 July, is Lille Ekkerøy. Unlike the others so far mentioned, this is on the south shore of the peninsula, inside the Varanger Fjord. Until quite recently it supported a farm, the ruined buildings of which are still surrounded by grassy hay-fields, and sheep are still grazed on the island in summer. Long ago, in the seventeenth century, it boasted a population which included 50 men. Although the same four species of gull nest here as on Kongsøya, they are in different proportions. There are only a very few kittiwakes. The flatter parts of the island are divided between common gulls, of which there are probably well over 200 pairs, making it perhaps the largest concentration of these birds in the Varanger Peninsula, and the two larger species, herring and greater black-backed gulls, which share the southern end of the island, leaving the northern to the common gulls.

The common gull colony on Lille Ekkeroy is perhaps rather atypical for the Varanger Peninsula, for the nests are placed on flattish grassy areas quite close together, and there are many of them. I could find only one common gull's nest with eggs, a clutch of two; but there were many chicks running about, their greyish mottled down making them very conspicuous in the lush grass. The common gull seems to breed in most parts of the Varanger Peninsula except the extensive stone-fields of the north. Inland, on the lower fells, it nests in small and scattered colonies by the lakes and in bogs. Along the coast it is a village bird; a few pairs only, usually being found in any one place, often quite scattered, sometimes single pairs only. The nests are sometimes on the roofs of outhouses, on piles of driftwood, or in the neighbouring hayfields. One bird was sitting on a nest on an upturned oildrum, just by the road, on the outskirts of one of the south coast villages. One wonders if these birds have become semi-domesticated in this way, to avoid predators like foxes. Neither man nor boy seem to molest them in the least bit.

Most numerous of all the gulls is certainly the kittiwake. There are many colonies round the shores of the peninsula besides the huge one at Syltefjord, some of them on mainland cliffs, as at Store Ekkerøy, where several thousand pairs breed on a quite low range of cliffs. Everywhere, I was told in the Varanger Peninsula, the kittiwake is increasing in numbers. It is probably extending its range too and new colonies are perhaps being founded. On 6 July I examined what appeared to be a recently-founded kittiwake colony; it certainly seems to be unrecorded in the literature. It was on the very low and easily climbable cliffs of Lille Ekkerøy. The birds were in two groups and almost all the nests could be examined at close quarters. The situation was as the table overleaf.

An unusual kittiwake colony is to be found in the harbour at Vardø where the birds nest on the window-ledges of old warehouses, just

	GROUP 1		GROUP 2
8 nests	2 eggs	*6 nests*	platform only
	1 egg, 1 chick	*5 platforms*	platform only
	1 egg, 1 chick	*or half-built nests*	platform only
	2 eggs		platform only
	1 egg		2 eggs
	2 eggs		2 eggs
	2 chicks		2 eggs
	2 eggs, 1 chick		1 egg
			2 chicks
			2 eggs
			platform only

Record of kittiwake colony, Lille Ekkerøy, 6 July.

like the well-known colony on the River Tyne in England. But, with a difference. Here at Vardø, in typically Scandinavian fashion, wooden ledges, or rather, open-fronted wooden nest-boxes, have been fixed to the walls for the kittiwakes' use. On two warehouses in the inner harbour about 50 pairs of kittiwakes were nesting, and there was another warehouse colony in the outer harbour numbering about 10–12 pairs.

The Arctic tern is one of the most attractive and easily observed of all the birds of the Varanger Peninsula. Colonies of 100 pairs or so are found all round the coast: on an island off Nesseby, at Saltjern, at Store Ekkerøy and on Lille Ekkerøy. Indeed there are three separate colonies on Lille Ekkerøy, numbering several hundred pairs in all. Only a few nests seemed to have hatched when I visited them on 6 July; most still had two eggs. At Saltjern the terns nest on the ground just outside the village, on either side of the road. Upwards of 100 pairs nest here, some in a marsh, some on gravelly waste ground by the road, some on dryish grassy ground and some on the shingle beach. It is a simple matter to stop one's car and watch and photograph these birds from it. Most were incubating clutches of two or three eggs when I inspected the colony on 10 June. They swooped at one's head and screamed into one's ear as one walked near their nests, and the villagers drawing water from, or washing clothes in, the stream, were also subjected to constant attack.

If you walk inland into the fells from the southern shore of the Varanger Peninsula anywhere beyond Vadsø you will come across breeding Arctic skuas. They breed from sea level – one pair nested in

1972 near the tip of Store Ekkerøy – up into the fells wherever the ground is covered with vegetation of a sort. The eggs I saw were laid on a carpet of crowberry and dwarf birch and many pairs of skuas had evidently included part of one of the dry rocky ridges in their territories. On such an outcrop the non-incubating bird of a pair would be seen standing as if on watch. Other pairs however had taken up residence in one of the tussocky bogs which are found all over the southern part of the peninsula. These birds are not found in the birch forest nor in the stone fields of the higher fells. The skua's two gull-like but surprisingly small eggs are relatively easy to find; the young are a very different matter. As for photography – the skua presents no problems. The hide is readily accepted and I was able to photograph both birds of a pair which had a nest on the fells above Golnes, in a single afternoon. In this case, one bird of the pair was a dark-phase bird and the other was light. Two boys from Vadsø, holidaying with relatives at Golnes, obligingly put me in my hide and walked away in a probably unnecessary attempt to allay the skuas' suspicions. Quite extraordinary, when you first come across it, is the injury feigning, or distraction display, of these birds. Standing on the ground, the skua spreads out and flutters its wings while emitting a thin, high-pitched note which is quite different from its usual loud 'yup yup'. It sounds rather like a small bird or mammal in distress. The human intruder's attention may well be deflected by this curious performance, but it does usually assure him that an occupied nest is near.

The Arctic skua is a big heavy bird with a superbly beautiful, buoyant, gliding flight. Even more elegant and masterful in the air is the rarer long-tailed skua which only breeds at all commonly in the Varanger Peninsula when lemmings are plentiful. It haunts the same fells as the Arctic skua but is usually found at a somewhat higher altitude. In the summer of 1972 few of these birds were nesting though one would come across groups of two or three birds here and there. It was not until 10 July that I found a pair that were evidently breeding, though I could not find the young birds which I suspected were hiding in jumbled boulders nearby. As I walked across the undulating fell, carpeted with the inevitable crowberry and dwarf birch, one of these long-tailed skuas came right up to me with a 'yup yup' note, flew round me, and settled near. Soon a second bird did the same and, as I continued my walk, their flights towards and around me became increasingly aggressive and demonstrative. Soon they were flying straight at my head, only swerving aside at the very last moment. They kept on flying round then diving down, then flying round again, yuppering angrily throughout the performance. They settled frequently and performed their distraction display, which was similar to the Arctic skua's. When I returned later the same thing happened, but one of the birds allowed me on several occasions to approach to within seven or eight metres of it while it stood on a rock or on the ground. When a third long-tailed skua flew over the area a loud 'ee-ow' calling started and the stranger indulged in a beautiful display flight, gliding with its wings arched downward. The long-tailed skua really is one of nature's grandest birds and one of the most attractive of all those fascinating species which inhabit the Scandinavian fells in summer.

The white wing-tips of this juvenile glaucous gull serve to identify it from the numerous herring gulls circling with it over the waters of Berlevåg harbour.

Looking east along the range of cliffs which afford nesting places for thousands of kittiwakes on the south shore of Store Ekkerøy. Far away to the left, on the distant horizon, is the southern end of the uninhabited island of Lille Ekkerøy, on which the author spent a day.

At Vardø, kittiwakes have taken up residence in the harbour and colonised a group of old warehouses. Many of the nests are on the ledges of boarded-up windows (above) *but the nest-boxes which have been put up specially for them are fully occupied too* (opposite).

The Arctic skua's two plumage phases, light and dark, may here be compared. These two birds were photographed on the same day at the same nest.

The change-over or relief ceremony at the nest of a pair of Arctic terns. The right-hand bird has just arrived and the incubating bird (left) has got up and is about to move off. Photographed at Saltjern on 11 June.

The Arctic skua's distraction display. The bird settles on the ground, spreads out and flaps its wings, and utters a series of high-pitched whispering calls while fixing the observer with a beady eye from over its shoulder.

The long-tailed skua is one of the most elegant and graceful of all the Varanger Peninsula's birds. This one, which allowed me to approach within a few metres of it, may have had young nearby, but many pairs were certainly not breeding in 1972, which was a poor lemming year.

Skuas in flight compared. The long-tailed skua has relatively longer and narrower wings and lacks the dark patch on the side of the Arctic skua's neck.

Some birds of fell and bog

6

Much of the ground inland from the northern shore of the Varanger Fjord and east of Vadsø and the limits of the birch forest, consists of low, undulating fell with occasional stony ridges, numerous bogs, and many lakes. Near Vadsø is one of the largest of these lakes, Langsmedvannet, and, immediately north of this lake lies the largest bog in the entire Varanger Peninsula, the redoubtable Kibymyr or marsh of Kiby. The whole of this area, unlike the stone deserts of the northern and higher parts of the peninsula, is relatively well covered with vegetation. Not only are crowberry and dwarf birch found nearly everywhere, but the bushy form of the common birch, and patches of scrub willow, are scattered throughout the area, especially along the river banks, while in the bogs there is a luxuriant growth of sphagnum moss, cotton-grass, sedge, and the like.

My first walk over these lower fells was on 13 June when I left the car at Saltjern and trudged northwards to Langsmedvannet. I passed several rocky ridges of smooth slabs and lichen encrusted boulders, the haunt of Arctic skuas and turnstones, but for the most part it was a flat, twiggy, almost prickly surface of lichen and dwarf birch over which one walked with ease. How different from our own heather-covered moors! Interspersed with the brilliant glossy green of the dwarf birch, the round sessile leaves of which were just appearing, was the reddish-brown and reddish-green of the crowberry, on which one could still find last year's berries, perfectly preserved by the winter's frost and quite edible. The marshy areas were slower to cross. Here there were often great soft squashy hummocks of sphagnum moss and peat, and patches of willow scrub.

On 21 June I spent the night on these fells in superb weather, approximately 2 km north of the southern shore of the peninsula. Here there was a marsh with willow and birch scrub; an outcrop of flat rocks; patches of dry crowberry-covered ground and a lovely view out over the Varanger Fjord. Above the distant snow-flecked and sunlit mountains on its southern shore were a few clouds. Below their summits a line of white mist separated them from the blue-grey waters of the fjord. The midnight sun shone with a clear, soft, hazy light which, however, made the wooden houses of the fishermen on distant Store Ekkerøy flash and sparkle. All around me the open expanse of fell lay ready to be explored.

The first bird which came to my attention in this area was the familiar golden plover. Not, however, familiar in every respect, for the northern form of the golden plover is a much more strikingly-patterned bird with a blacker breast bordered by a more continuous and conspicuous white line, than the golden plover of our moors. I noticed other differences, too. The golden plovers here were almost invariably in the marshier terrain, not on the dry tops, though the species extends up to 400 m provided there is suitable boggy or peaty ground, and downwards almost to sea level. Areas of peaty tussocks are particularly favoured and the birds love to perch on top of these. Though it must be reckoned one of the commoner breeding waders of the Varanger Peninsula, the golden plover is certainly not found in such dense concentrations as, for example, in parts of the North Yorkshire moors. Flocking in the Varanger Peninsula starts early: on 9 July I counted over twenty together, apparently all adults, near Hanglefjell. One nest I found was in a situation typical of many: on the top of one of the big hummocks of peat already referred to. Its three eggs were somewhat different in colour to those of English birds, lacking any chocolate or reddish tinge in the spots and blotches. They merged superbly with the lichen and moss growing round them. The bird would sit tight, tighter than its southern counterpart, then scuffle off the nest, flutter a few yards only and start deliberate injury feigning. On one occasion it kept up this extraordinary performance, with head held low, outstretched wings and depressed, fanned out tail, for ten minutes or more, sometimes lying spreadeagled and completely still, sometimes fluttering one or both wings. Most of these movements were slow and deliberate. Another bird flushed from a clutch of eggs on 4 July flew off with a low, unsure, injury-feigning flight, looking for all the world like some queer water bird or injured grouse.

Commonest of all the peninsula's breeding waders is undoubtedly the dunlin, though its choice of habitat seems restricted to the bogs. On all of these, however, it is numerous, more so than the golden plover. It was on 23 June that I saw my first dunlin chicks, which had probably hatched early that morning or the night before. With their white spots and warm brown down mottled with black, newly hatched dunlins are among the most attractive of waders. They are also extraordinarily well camouflaged especially when, as here, they were squatting among dwarf birch twigs, lichen and above all, dead leaves, in this case of the cloudberry plant. One of the adult birds stood anxiously on a hummock of sphagnum moss not 10 m from me, calling loudly with its curious rasping alarm note 'quy quy', as well as a shrill 'shreep'. The dunlin's breeding season is relatively prolonged for waders: I found another nest with the chicks still in it on 10 July. It was a depression in a marsh, partly concealed by dwarf birch and willow and lined with pieces of dry sedge. Both adults were present. One had been brooding the chicks; the other was standing a few metres away. The dunlin's song flight was one of the most characteristic bird songs of the peninsula and I often watched this delightful performance. A bird would fly up, then glide downwards with a downward pointing bill, uttering a squeaky trill that rises, then falls, in pitch and intensity.

Other waders which nest in the bogs among the fells are the two species of stint, but these will be considered in a later chapter. The wood sandpiper also prefers this habitat but seemed to be breeding only rather sparsely, though its 'chip chip chip' or 'chirroo chirroo' songs, uttered as it flies high over its breeding territory, carried far and wide. A pair not far from Vadsø certainly had young out of the nest, but well hidden in the marsh, on 4 July. One bird flew about to and fro over my head calling excitedly 'chiff chiff chiff' and repeatedly perching on the dwarf willow bushes that grew here and there in this expanse of bog, which the wood sandpipers shared with at least one pair of common snipe.

A passerine bird that is a very numerous inhabitant of the Varanger Peninsula's bogs is the Lapland bunting. Even a small bog would harbour several pairs, and these charming birds were also found in drier areas of peat, for example on Store Ekkerøy, but never on the dry open fells. They need some bushes or low trees on which to perch, or at least hummocks of peat, and the nests, which were not difficult to find when they contained young, were well hidden in the bog vegetation, often in the side of a tussock among dwarf birch, cloudberry and other plants. The male Lapland bunting, with its black head and chestnut nape, is a striking and attractive bird which allows quite close approach. Both birds of a pair feed the young, visiting the nest every few minutes with caterpillars. The earliest date that came to my notice on which young left the nest was 21 June. Sometimes at least, they leave the nest before they can fly, like shorelarks and probably other ground-nesting passerines. I photographed a pair which were feeding young still in the nest on 22 and 23 June. They were confiding and entertaining birds which perched near the nest calling 'tee-u' and 'cheep'. While I was in the hide I induced distraction display in the male by placing a black focussing cloth on the ground in front of the hide. He called 'eek eek eek' – a note I once heard a female make as she fluttered off a nest – and spread out his wings and lowered his tail, but soon returned to his normal sprightly and apparently fearless self.

The bogs of the Varanger fells ought not to be passed by without a word about the most extensive of them all, Kibymyr, situated only a few kilometres from Vadsø. Jostein Grastveit was making a special study of its birds and I walked through a small part of it with him on 22 June and again on 28 June. This immense marsh appeared to be rounded or dome-shaped rather than flat. The surface, which is studded with lakes, consists of patches of sedgy bog interspersed with dry peaty mounds and ridges. It is difficult 'up and down' walking and an exhausting five-mile trudge would be necessary to cover its whole length. It seems possible that jack-snipe and bar-tailed godwits may breed here in some years. Dunlin and golden plovers are quite common and there are many pairs of Lapland buntings. There is an abundance of insect life here, including a quite notable concentration of mosquitoes.

On the open drier fells the meadow pipit was common wherever the vegetation was thick enough to conceal its nest. Here and there a pair of turnstones, sometimes ringed plovers, would be found on a stony ridge, and wheatears and snow buntings occurred wherever there were rocks. The handsome willow grouse, the exact counterpart and very close relative of the English or Scottish red grouse except for its white wings, was present but was by no means common. By far the most conspicuous and characteristic breeding bird of these lower fells, carpeted with dwarf birch, lichen and crowberry, was the whimbrel. Not that it could be described as really common. Indeed no species was really common; birds of any kind were sparse in these immense empty wastes between the lakes and bogs.

It was on 26 June that I found my first whimbrel's nest after a long watch, during which it became clear that one bird normally remained 'on guard' on a rocky ridge while its mate incubated. This nest was in a most unusual situation, in a thick clump of vegetation forming a tiny islet in a small lake. A more typical nest was found on 27 June and photographed on 29 June when the eggs were chipped and nearly ready to hatch. It was a beautiful nest in the open tundra, surrounded by lichen, though there was a sprig of dwarf birch just next to it, and some crowberry. Photography from a hide was a simple matter and I had no need of an assistant to accompany me to the hide and then walk away. Within a few minutes of my entering the hide one of these stately birds, apparently paler or sandier in colour than a curlew, with lovely grey legs, was walking about near the nest; soon it stepped confidently up to the nest, and settled to incubate the four beautifully mottled eggs. The other bird of the pair stood about on a ridge, very upright, not 30 m away. There is something extremely elegant and lovely about the whimbrel's slow deliberate gait. It is a more balanced, less clumsy bird, than the curlew. Its call is a clear loud bubbling trill, made from the ground, but more often in flight, which in its more elaborate form sometimes begins almost exactly like a curlew's. Unfortunately time did not permit me to remain to watch and photograph these whimbrels hatch. When I left on 29 June two eggs were emitting a soft, sweet, prolonged whistling call and two little beaks could be seen moving through holes in the shell.

The whimbrel, which shared the same ground as the Arctic skua in places, prefers those parts of the fell with a peatier soil and some vegetation on the ground. Besides the ever-present redpoll, at least two passerines were to be found in these fells commonly enough, but only where bushes were present: the bluethroat, favouring birch scrub, and the red-throated pipit, favouring willow scrub. Both species, especially the latter, seemed to be commoner near the coast, the south coast in particular. The Dutch birdwatcher, Hidde Bult, showed me a bluethroat's nest on 14 June, deeply hidden in a mossy bank. It was screened by dwarf birch, with globe flowers and cranes-bill growing just by it, and it contained seven pale blue eggs. The bluethroat is certainly the finest songster in the Varanger Peninsula and probably the most colourful bird, for the intense blue of the male's breast has to be seen to be believed. But this robin-like species has another and quite different claim to distinction: it is the only bird which more or less poses to have its photograph taken! At any rate this pair was extremely obliging in this respect. They perched on twigs at just the right distance from the hide, and they stayed there while two or three exposures were made. Particularly when a bird was approached by its mate it would indulge in a brief tail-flicking display, partly opening the wings at the same time. Actually the two birds seldom remained together; one or other of them was at or near the nest almost continuously and both visited it with insects every few minutes. The bluethroat is a slim, rather long-legged and long-tailed bird with a whitish eye-stripe; something of a cross between a warbler and a robin, with a 'tack tack' alarm note. The rufous on either side of the base of the tail and the rufous under tail coverts give it a touch of colour as it flits away through the bushes.

The other bush-loving passerine of the lower fells is the red-throated pipit, a largish pipit of variable colour in summer but often with a pronounced reddish-buff tinge on throat and breast. It actually nests on the ground, but probably always near bushes, on which it habitually perches. I spent hours watching a pair near Krampenes on 5 and 7 July, but even though I erected a hide and watched them from it, I never succeeded in finding their nest, which certainly contained young and which was situated in a clearing in a patch of willow scrub. Hitherto I had reckoned a tree pipit's nest with young one of the very hardest to find; now the red-throated pipit takes pride of place. The male of this pair was spotted only on the flanks; his throat and upper breast were pinkish-red; the lower breast buff coloured. The female had a reddish-brown throat but was quite boldly spotted on the breast. Both birds were tall, large and handsome with striking pink legs and feet. When disturbed, they called constantly 'cheep cheep' both from the air and when perched. This anxiety note was easily distinguished from the 'tsip tsip' note of a neighbouring pair of meadow pipits. Both pipits are widely distributed over the fells of the Varanger Peninsula, the red-throated perhaps commoner along the coast, where the rock pipit also occurs in suitable localities.

The golden plover of the Varanger Peninsula belongs to the brightly-coloured northern race of that species. Standing upright near the nest, its black and white plumage pattern is more conspicuous than that of the average southern bird.

An anxious dunlin perches near its newly-hatched chicks on a peaty hummock covered with lichen and dwarf birch.

Taken out of its natural surroundings and placed on the photographer's notebook (bottom) *the day-old dunlin chick becomes a quite conspicuous object. This bird was found crouching just by its nest on 23 June* (top).

Abundant in all the Varanger Peninsula's many bogs and peaty areas is the Lapland bunting. Below: *A male droops its wings in a distraction display in response to the appearance of a black focussing cloth outside the author's hide.* Bottom: *Bird photographers usually open up nests so as to make the bird visible and the nest quite unnaturally open. Here a male Lapwing bunting merges with the cloudberry and dwarf birch leaves which surround the well hidden nest, which has not been tampered with at all. The open beaks of three young birds are visible in it.*

Opposite: *An anxious wood sandpiper, with young in a marsh near Vadsø, perches on a sprig of birch near the intruder.*

The whimbrel is one of the commonest and most attractive breeding waders of the Varanger fells. This nest, typically, was a depression in lichen and dwarf birch and contained four eggs which were almost ready to hatch when this photograph was taken on 29 June.

The bluethroat, perched near the nest after feeding its young, reacts to the near presence of its mate by hunching its body and partly spreading its wings and tail.

A female red-throated pipit among grass and dwarf birch photographed from a hide near its nest, which was not however found. This pipit is tall and handsome with pink legs and varying amounts of reddish on its throat in the breeding season.

Two species of grouse Lagopus *inhabit the Varanger Peninsula, the willow grouse* (top), *which is the same species as our so-called red grouse, and the ptarmigan* (above). *Both are widespread though nowadays neither can be described as common; many fall prey to the local sportsmen. The ptarmigan lives on the bare tops and ridges, extending downwards to below 100 m in the stony northern fells; the willow grouse is a bird of the lower fells. Both species are white in winter but are shown here in their very similar summer plumage.*

Sørfjell and Hanglefjell

7

The fells of the Varanger Peninsula are neither especially striking nor particularly high. There is little rugged mountain scenery, few crags and cliffs, no notable peaks. Nonetheless, on their bare flat tops is a strange world of unusual beauty, tinted in subtle colours by the varying hues of stone and lichen, scarred and fragmented by the freezing forces of the savage winter climate, and inhabited, sparsely enough, by a handful of remarkable birds, in particular the snow bunting, ptarmigan and dotterel. When I first arrived in the peninsula these tops were still covered with immense snowfields but, by the end of June, the heat-wave had removed a great deal of the snow and even dried up the streams on Sørfjell. Then, in the stifling heat of that exceptional summer, the tops became a brassy, stony desert, only occasionally cooled by a passing thunder shower. This is how I found Sørfjell on 2 July; and Hanglefjell, though higher and further north, was no different on 8 July.

Jostein Grastveit had told me that he had once found breeding dotterels on Sørfjell above Nesseby. In order to look for birds there, it was necessary to take camping equipment and stay at least one night on or near the summit plateau. A march of some eight miles either way was involved, and the youthful birdwatcher of Nesseby, Sverre A. Nilsen, jumped at the opportunity to accompany me on what was his first expedition into the fells. He shared my tent but brought his own food and equipment, which included cold polsers or sausages, two dictionaries, a bird book, a fearsomely sharp and wicked-looking camping-knife, together with some elastoplast against a possible mishap with it, supplies of anti-mosquito oil, a box camera and a superb pair of 7×50 Russian binoculars. I was heavily laden too.

It was a sweltering hot day as we set out through the birch woods of the Maskelv valley at 0830 hours and I could not resist the temptation, when we reached the upper reaches of the river some two and a half hours later, of taking off my clothes and splashing into and sitting in its cooling waters. Camp was pitched at midday, of necessity some distance below the summit because the entire top of the mountain was completely devoid of water. Indeed the whole of the upper course of the nearest stream had dried up. We camped near the highest shallow pool, several hundred metres above the first deep clear pool of good drinking water, and even further from the first actual running water. As we trudged upwards during the morning a small white cloud over the fells slowly grew in a perfectly blue sky until at last, as we were preparing our midday meal, the scorching sun went in and a delightful breeze cooled us. Later on this same cloud rumbled out some thunder and shed a few drops of rain, while others towered upwards along the south shore of the Varanger Fjord.

In the evening these clouds dispersed. As I sat outside the tent I overlooked a splendid panorama of mile after mile of rolling fell. Immediately in front of me the ground sloped downwards to the valley of the River Maskelv far below. Beyond it, and beyond some further fells, I could see the dark green birch forest we had walked through that morning. In the far distance, leftwards, was the Varanger Fjord; to the right a distant, sombre, flat-topped line of fells was lit by the brilliant evening sun which cast a soft hazy light over the whole of this magnificent mountain landscape. All around me was an immense swarm of whirring mosquitoes making all sorts of notes and noises – an infernal insect orchestra which eventually drove one to seek refuge in the tent. At 2130 hours when we turned in, it was delightfully cool, but at 0300 hours, when I woke, a hot sun was climbing well up the sky, making the inside of the tent stiflingly hot. As I lay on the groundsheet in nothing but pants – it was too hot to lie on a sleeping-bag – I listened to the monstrous hum of a thousand mosquitoes outside the tent; they caused a constant pitter-patter just like rain, as they settled on to, and took off from, the roof of the tent.

The birds of Sørfjell, which is, as its name implies, the most southerly fell of the peninsula, were few and far between. On the afternoon of 2 July Sverre and I tramped over the bare, flat, stony tops above our camp but came across only a single pair of ptarmigans, and a single pair of snow buntings feeding young in a nest under a large boulder. Once or twice a dotterel flew past high over our heads with its curious 'plip plip plip' call; a solitary long-tailed skua was present but evidently not breeding, and not far below the tops there were golden plovers and an occasional dunlin and turnstone. Once a redpoll flew past us calling – a bird which I met with in almost every part of the Varanger Peninsula.

The snow buntings I resolved to photograph there and then. The hide was soon fetched from the camp and moved up in stages during the afternoon, the birds apparently ignoring it completely. I began photographing at 1600 hours, at a range of 12 m, and later moved the hide up to 2½ m. It was hot and dead calm on that flat desert of stones; seldom have I been so hot in a hide, but, from 1700 hours onwards a delicate breeze wafted a thousand sweet scents into the hide through the front peep-hole. Even though it was on a flat stony plateau 450 m above the sea, the mosquitoes buzzed infernally inside the hide. When near the nest, the adult snow buntings uttered a curious 'zizz zizz' call like a morse buzzer. While the female's approach to the nest was furtive and almost in part subterranean, the male preferred to perch openly on the lichen-covered boulders. Caterpillars and various insects were brought to the nest and the birds certainly found most of this food near at hand.

The next morning Sverre and I began to search in earnest for breeding dotterels. Keeping twenty or so paces apart, we crunched over the brick-coloured stones in long straight lines and wide circles. To and fro everywhere we trudged on these vast flat ridges and summits. Almost at the outset, we found two dotterels which flew right away when we approached them and seemed not to have a nest. It was only after more than two hours of walking with eyes constantly searching the ground ahead, that we eventually spotted a dotterel creeping away from us some twenty paces away. We stopped to watch it; it stood still, as if in a trance, while I photographed it with a 500 mm mirror lens on a tripod and Sverre scrutinised it delightedly with his bright crisp Russian binoculars. At last it walked away from me. I went back to Sverre and we settled down to watch it. It advanced towards us, sometimes walking, sometimes running, until suddenly it settled on what was obviously a nest. In this enormous flat wilderness of rock we had somehow contrived to find the tiny bird – smaller than a golden plover – and the nest for which we were looking. For an hour we stayed at or near it, and the bird which had left its nest furtively when we were twenty or thirty paces from it, now sat tight on its three rounded eggs, heavily mottled with black. If disturbed by a hand extended too near, it merely walked off a few metres, then returned to its eggs, stopping now and then to spread its tail or wing while turning away from us: a slightly-developed distraction display which was sometimes accompanied by a loud 'pee pee' call.

Sørfjell, with its snow buntings, ptarmigans and dotterels, even if they are but sparsely distributed, even if the tops are barren and partly devoid of vegetation, is definitely a bird locality, a place where one felt one would see and find something. Hanglefjell, exactly 25 km due north as the crow flies and 150 m higher, is surprisingly different. It was mentioned in the literature as a place where purple sandpipers had been found (Schmidt, 1967), but since this author had reported them also on Store Ekkerøy where I could find no trace of them whatsoever and since I had failed to find Hanglefjell on the map, I was by no means hopeful of finding them there. What decided me to go was the discovery, which I made on one of my visits to the baths at Vadsø, that Hanglefjell was the very same mountain which I had admired from the road, when it was still snow-covered, as I drove to Kongsøya on 16 June. Then, its delicately coloured grey rocks had been wreathed in massive snow drifts, producing an extraordinarily lovely pattern of grey and white. I resolved to make an expedition there, and the evening of 7 July found me installed by the Arctic Ocean Highway,

5 km south-east of the summit of Hanglefjell as the crow flies. Now, this mile-long hump of grey rock, which rises to 618 m in height, was nearly devoid of snow save for one long drift from top to bottom. No vegetation was visible on this bare stone desert but behind me, to the south of the road, the fells were green, and near at hand a redwing sang in the willow scrub along the banks of a small river. It was calm, clear, warm and extraordinarily peaceful.

Leaving the car next morning at 0845 hours, I reached the majestic ridge of steeply inclined grey rock slabs at 1030 after clambering over a series of steep humps of jumbled grey boulders. The weather was beautiful: sun, from a clear blue sky; then a few small cumulus clouds and, always, a cooling breeze. From the ridge a superb cloud-shadow-dappled fell landscape extended all round. Predominantly green to the south, northwards its colour was pale buff with soft shades of brown and grey. In that direction, it was a stone desert, stretching as far as the eye could see. The top of the ridge I was now on was just a heap of large sharp-edged boulders, but its south-east face was beautifully sheer and smooth. Below it was a chain of small lakes. I headed across the plateau towards the main summit, over stony flats, coming across patches of fine whitish sand. Here the boulders were worn smooth, even rounded, perhaps by blown sand. I made my way up to the summit cairn of Hanglefjell over a tangled mass of big reddish rock slabs and boulders. The top of the mountain is a boulder desert: no place for a walker, especially as many of the boulders are loose. Thereafter I trudged over the rocks for some hours; across the stone desert which occupies so much of the northern part of the Varanger Peninsula. The landscape's subtle beauty is due to the various delicate stone hues of grey, pinkish and buff, and the play of light and shade. It is beautiful, but utterly lonely and desolate. No vegetation grows here save lichen. No birds were encountered on Hanglefjell itself. An occasional ghostly cheep might have been a bird, but in fact it was my rucksack, which had a squeak something like the call of a juvenile snow bunting. All day long I had traversed a terrain of stones which, it seemed, could only be crossed by a hungry reindeer or a determined human being.

It was only when I had at last returned to the rocky valley far below that I encountered my first birds since early that morning: a snow bunting and a raven. Then, a few minutes later, as I followed the course of the stream downhill, I heard an unfamiliar note. It was a loud, sudden human-like whistling 'tweet', which almost took my breath away in that silent empty wilderness. A moment later I spotted the bird, perched on a boulder, with upright, anxious, stance. It was the elusive purple sandpiper. Withdrawing across the stream and up the hillside opposite I watched for a long time until a second bird appeared. Both seemed interested in a particular piece of ground and, when this was searched, a single young bird was found, perhaps two days out of the nest, crouching absolutely still by a boulder.

The breeding habitat of the purple sandpiper was about 350 m above sea level in a river valley, about a kilometre above the first of a series of flat, swampy areas which flanked the stream lower down. It was dry rocky ground; an undulating area of grey boulders with a thin growth of crowberry and dwarf birch in the spaces between them, and some grass, especially near the river. While I examined and photographed the purple sandpiper chick, the adult from time to time flew up and settled near me, coming as close as two metres. Then it would hurry away, tail down, feathers ruffled into a ball, creeping close to the ground. This was the famous rodent run, one of the most elaborate examples, among birds, of a distraction display. Sometimes, immediately after settling near me and before running off, it shook itself violently so that it resembled a big fluffy ball, calling at the same time. If you followed this rodent run, the bird ran all the more. Next morning I searched the area again but, finding no trace of the birds, I stripped and dived into the river where a deep pool with a sandy bottom showed as a patch of clear greenish-blue. It was an extremely hot day, but the breeze, though warm and not in the least bit cooling, was strong enough to keep mosquitoes out of action. As I finished my bathe and clambered out on the bank I heard the 'wheet' of a purple sandpiper perched on a boulder near me. I spent the next hour photographing this charming bird, which as it sat on a boulder, repeatedly allowed me to approach within 6–8 m with a telephoto lens mounted on a tripod. No thought of putting on clothes entered my head: that morning's photography was undertaken while I was stark naked and, when eventually I had secured pictures of the purple sandpiper in both colour and black-and-white, I plunged once again into the deliciously refreshing waters of that mountain stream.

Opposite: *Beyond the dark-blue waters of a mountain stream, near which Temminck's stints and a pair of purple sandpipers were nesting, rises the stony south ridge of Hanglefjell.*

Below: *A male snow bunting near its nest under a boulder on one of the summit ridges of Sørfjell.*

Bottom: *A dotterel settles onto its three eggs on Sørfjell.*

The stony wastes of Hanglefjell. In boulder deserts such as this one the only vegetation is sparse lichen, and the going for the walker is hard.

Below: *The parent purple sandpiper stands alertly upright on a lichen-covered boulder while its chick* (opposite, bottom), *superbly camouflaged with a lichen-like pattern on its downy back, crouches quite still beside a rock.*

Below: *A purple sandpiper creeps along with its feathers ruffled and its body hunched, performing its distraction display which is designed to lure the intruder away from its nest or young.*

Phalaropes and stints

8

Although the grey phalarope breeds in Iceland and Spitsbergen, on Bear Island and probably Kolguev, and eastwards from the Taymyr Peninsula on the Siberian mainland, it is unknown in the Varanger Peninsula. On the other hand the red-necked phalarope is one of the most characteristic and attractive of the peninsula's breeding birds. Not only can a pair or two, or even a colony several pairs strong, be found by many an inland pool throughout the peninsula, but flocks frequent a series of shallow pools along the Varanger Fjord throughout the summer.

The phalarope turned out to be the first bird I photographed in the Varanger Peninsula, for I found up to fifteen of them feeding on the pool, which is a well-known locality for them, on the grassy promontory just by Nesseby church, where I camped in the car on my first night by the Varanger Fjord, 8 June. The next morning I drove the car to near the edge of the pool and spent some hours watching and photographing the phalaropes, which were tame enough, if you kept still, to approach within two or three metres. It was a windy and cold but brilliantly clear and sunny morning. I sat in the car on the east side of the pool sheltered from the freezing wind from that direction and warmed by the sun. In front of me was the dark blue wind-rippled phalarope pool with, beyond, a green weed-grown fringe in which the phalaropes loved to feed. Beyond that, a strip of bright green grass separated the pool from the intense blue waters of the Varanger Fjord. Above, in the pale blue sky, an unending procession of common terns and kittiwakes flew up towards me and passed by close overhead, heading straight into the wind. The phalaropes never ceased their intense activity. Either they were feeding or preening or dashing about in little parties, flying at each other and alighting near each other with a splash, repeating their short 'twick twick' notes. When a pair was seen swimming together one would often notice that the more brightly-coloured female was swimming after and more or less chasing her mate. Sometimes a male bobbed up and down in the water, showing his white belly; sometimes a bird made a loud whirring noise with its wings directly after taking flight. By crawling over the sheep-cropped turf and the ice-smoothed boulders, which were coloured in places with brilliant orange lichen, I found I could very easily photograph these phalaropes at close quarters.

On 23 June, on my next visit to the Nesseby phalarope pool, I counted 28 phalaropes there, and there may have been as many as 50; but there were none at all there on 3 and 4 July; nor did I see a single bird on my last visit on 15 July. But similar flocks were seen at similar pools along the Varanger shore. For example, on the island on which part of Vadsø is now built is the pool from which Vadsø took its name, literally the island with a pool on it (*Vatnsoy* or *Oen med Vannet*). Here on 20 June Jostein Grastveit and I counted 38 phalaropes, most of which he thought were females; and on 29 June at the eastern end of Store Ekkerøy, on a very similar pool, I counted 39 birds. Red-necked phalaropes were also frequently met with along the shore of the Varanger Fjord throughout my stay. On 6 July I encountered a charming compact flock of 30 birds which were feeding on the sea, but also on some rock pools margined with green slime. They split up into tight little groups of 10 or 15 birds, bobbing up and down on the water and spiralling round or spinning, and often flying up and along the shore. Some of these birds had lost much of their red colour; one was already almost in winter plumage.

Though on 10 June, at Saltjern, I had watched red-necked phalaropes copulating in the water of a tiny stream, the female completely submerged save for her head, I never found a nest of these birds. A month later, however, on 10 July, after a prolonged search, I found and photographed a phalarope chick which was probably only one day old – a tiny, fragile, stripy speck of life concealed in a dense sedge jungle on the edge of a pool inland among the Varanger fells.

The two European species of stint both breed in the Varanger Peninsula but, while Temminck's stint is common and widespread throughout the area, the little stint is much rarer. Indeed it has not yet been proved to breed regularly every year, and in some localities it has certainly only nested sporadically. Since the little stint is a rare bird, and very easily disturbed, it is perhaps just as well that the few cases of proved breeding in the Varanger Peninsula have not been particularly well documented in the literature. What does seem deplorable, however, is that at least two of these important records have been published first in *British Birds* instead of *Sterna*. Why cannot English bird-watchers and editors of journals give a little more thought to the problem of which is the best and most suitable place to publish such records? I was once reproved by a well-known English ornithologist for publishing my discovery of dotterels' breeding in Italy in the *Rivista italiana di ornitologia*: it should have been in an English journal! But to return from this digression; the following published records of little stints breeding in the Varanger Peninsula are known to me:

7 July 1965	Nest with 4 eggs on Vadsøya (Jennings, 1966)
30 July 1967	Adult with chick near Hamningberg (Haftorn, 1971)
7 July 1968	Nest with 4 eggs on Store Ekkerøy (Ferguson-Lees, 1969, Risberg, 1972)

10 July 1971	Nest with 4 eggs, Vesterdal near Kongsfjord (Risberg, 1972)
15 June 1971	Nest with 8 eggs, but later robbed (Reynolds, 1972)

In 1972 little stints were seen, and heard trilling, at some of the above localities and elsewhere, and on 11 July I came across a bird which kept returning to the same piece of ground, called anxiously 'tip tip tip', and allowed me to approach it closely. After watching it for some time I realised that it had young dispersed in the marsh nearby, but I did not undertake the systematic search which would have been necessary to find them for fear of adding to the risk of inadvertently treading on one of these fragile creatures. Instead, I contented myself with photographing the adult bird.

The Temminck's stint is common in many parts of the Varanger Peninsula and in June its beautiful trilling song-flight was very much in evidence. A bird would alight after this flight on a roadside post and continue trilling there. On Vadsøya two or three could be seen and heard, sometimes nearly hovering, uttering their minute-long clear trills as they flew about 20 or 30 feet above the ground in this special display flight. Many pairs nested in the coastal hayfields, but marshes inland in the fells and boggy river-valleys everywhere, were also occupied by Temminck's stints.

It was on 9 July that I found a Temminck's stint's nest on an inland marsh which contained two dry chicks and one still wet, and a single egg. It was found after I had located the bird by its 'trick trick' alarm note and watched it for some time; it really was the smallest and best camouflaged nest I have ever seen. Partly under a dwarf willow in a patch of the same plants, it was 3 m from a river bank and some 10 m from a large sedgy marsh. Under my very eyes, the two older chicks, and then the third, left the nest and followed the adult away. By keeping still I was able to watch and photograph the adult stint with its brood from a distance of 8-10 m or less. The parent ran mouse-like through the sedges and dwarf willows, contriving, with what seemed to be amazing skill, an almost invisible approach to its chicks. It brooded them within a few paces of me but also called them gradually further away with a gentle trilling note. It was relatively tame, or fearless, though not so much so as many other Temminck's stints at hatching time.

The thin, silvery trill of the Temminck's stint is one of the most attractive and characteristic bird sounds of the Varanger Peninsula but it is hard to appreciate how very small this tiny wader and its relative, the little stint, really are. As a matter of fact, at five inches in length, they are somewhat smaller than a robin. It is a curious fact that, though Temminck's stint is common in many parts of Norway and the little stint is only found sparsely in the extreme north-east, yet as migrants in England the little stint is not uncommon while Temminck's is distinctly rare. Evidently they tend to migrate in different directions though they may be seen together in Jutland in August as well as in the Varanger Peninsula in June and July.

Over Vadsøya a Temminck's stint performs its prolonged, trilling song-flight.

Red-necked phalarope pairs photographed on 9 June at Nesseby. Swimming through the water, the female gently pursues the male.

On the grassy bank of the pool the more brightly-coloured female is on the left. In the phalaropes, the traditional roles of the sexes are reversed: the duller-coloured male performs most of the domestic duties, including incubation.

A red-necked phalarope flock in flight.

The little stint is probably a regular though sparsely distributed breeder in the Varanger Peninsula. This bird, which had young in an inland marsh, allowed me to approach close to it and repeatedly flew up and settled close to me.

Hayfields, villages and the shore

9

So far we have considered some of the wilder parts of the Varanger Peninsula, but humans have lived there for 9,000 years and human settlement has left an enduring impact on the coastal landscape, especially in the south, along the Varanger shore. All the towns and villages are in fact on the coast, and so are virtually all the permanently occupied habitations, though the interior of the peninsula is scattered with, and its beauty often spoilt by, numerous wooden huts which are used mainly in the summer. The crop invariably associated with human settlement is hay, and the small rectangular fenced-in hayfields are a characteristic feature of the settled areas throughout the peninsula.

A few species of bird are found only in, or are closely associated with, the human settlements. The magpie, for example, is a typical village bird and nests may be found only a few feet up in birch or willow scrub, often by a road or track. At Store Ekkerøy I saw a nest constructed of wire built on the side of one of the houses. The hooded crow, too, frequents human habitation and nests on power-line pylons and fish-drying racks as well as in trees. I found an occupied nest in a birch tree in Vadsø churchyard but had not the courage to climb up. One nest I did go up to, though it proved to be empty, was a bizarre affair built of string, sticks, seaweed, wire, barbed wire and fish back-bones! It was, as it were, right out to sea, perched on the navigation light at the end of the jetty at Store Ekkerøy harbour.

The starling has scarcely reached the Varanger Peninsula, having bred only at Nesseby in a hole in the wooden church there, at Nyborg, and one or two other places, including a nestbox in Vadsø; but the house sparrow has colonised most of the villages, including Vadsø and Berlevåg. I have refrained, however, from including its photograph in this book. The white wagtail is another typical village bird. One bird which seems to be confined to hayfields, but is found all over the peninsula wherever there are any, is the skylark. I recorded it all along the south coast as well as at several places in the north, including Syltefjord and Berlevåg.

Several species of wader breed in the hayfields but are also found elsewhere, on marshy ground: the redshank, curlew and ruff. All three are commonest near the coast. On 12 June I found a redshank's nest with four eggs in the corner of an abandoned hayfield on Store Ekkerøy. It was 3 m from the fence round the edge of the field and only 10 m from the track bordering it. It was a little surprising to find curlews nesting in these small fields, though they were by no means common. After a search on 23 June Jostein Grastveit and I, helped by Sverre and Willi, found and ringed a well-grown young curlew at Nesseby. The adult birds circled round yelling loudly and one of them kept swooping down to within a few metres of us when we were handling its chick.

I had hoped, during my first few days in the Varanger Peninsula, to photograph the ruffs which Blair had long ago observed displaying and fighting on heaps of seaweed along the shore. But there were no heaps of seaweed, and no ruffs on the shore. Instead, I found that the ruff was a typical hayfield bird, though it was common enough too in marshy ground, mostly coastal but also inland. When I first arrived, in the second week of June, ruffs were very much in evidence at Nesseby, Paddeby, Saltjern, Store Ekkerøy and other south coast localities. They could be seen in small flocks in the hayfields, their variegated plumage making them for all the world like domestic chickens. The size of each lek varied, but about fifteen birds seemed normal.

It was on the edge of the small marsh by the village of Saltjern that I put up a hide near the grassy knoll where the local ruffs were lekking. For the ruffs, it was in fact late in the season, and they spent much of their time either standing quite still on a hummock in the marsh, or walking about the marsh feeding, making subdued gobbling noises. Only every now and then did they gather on the lekking-place for one of their bizarre, excited scuffles. First they seemed to be rushing about madly in all directions. Then two individuals would lunge at one another in mock battle and one would suddenly sprawl on the ground with fluffed-out feathers while its opponent would stand triumphantly over it, pointing its bill threateningly downwards, and walk to and fro round it, always keeping its head towards the bird lying prone. Sometimes two ruffs would lie quite still, sprawled out on the ground. The reeve meanwhile would creep about submissively nearby. Then suddenly, all the birds would fly off. Unfortunately I could spare only a few hours to study and photograph these unusual and fascinating birds, which are one of the most characteristic waders of the Varanger Peninsula.

The shores of the Varanger Peninsula afford suitable breeding and feeding places for many waders. Of those which do not breed, the bar-tailed godwit is one of the most attractive. In spite of the presence of large summering flocks of these birds, often in their spectacular red summer plumage, and of paired and even apparently courting birds along the shore, the bar-tailed godwit is at best only a very rare breeder on one or two inland marshes. Early on the morning of 12 June I found one feeding on the north shore of Store Ekkerøy, which, loath to fly away when I approached it, stood on a rock facing me and called loud and long 'er-quaper-quape er-quip'. But usually these were shy and retiring birds which were seen at their best, perhaps, when feeding at Nesseby at low tide.

Of breeding shore waders in the Varanger Peninsula there are three species: the oystercatcher, ringed plover and turnstone. Not that the last two of these are by any means confined to the shore – far from it. Both ringed plovers and turnstones also breed in scattered pairs and colonies far inland in the fells, especially in the southern part of the peninsula, on suitable stony patches of ground. On 27 June I found a pair of turnstones with young a few kilometres inland from Golnes and was interested to discover that the greyish young bird, which was just starting to grow feathers, seemed to prefer to hide in the scanty vegetation, which was mainly dwarf birch, rather than freeze among the stones like a ringed plover chick.

The densest concentrations of turnstones were perhaps on the stony crowberry heath which backed the shore in some places, notably on the north side of Store Ekkerøy. Here, on gently sloping ground above the boulder-strewn beach is an extensive area of crowberry heath interspersed with boulders and patches of dry lichen-covered stony ground. Several pairs of turnstones were breeding here side by side. Sometimes two birds would have a territorial combat, stretching their heads upwards then bowing them low in a curious bobbing movement. If a nest was approached, the incubating bird would fly off when one was still 30 m or more away; then suddenly appear on a rock close at hand but some distance from the nest, calling loudly 'peeu wheeter wheeter wheeter wee tee tee tu'. This behaviour made the nests hard to find, but there was little difficulty if one was lucky enough to mark the spot where the bird first took wing, for these Varanger Peninsula nests were all quite open, not concealed under a rock or in a hole as often elsewhere. The eggs were very olive-green in general tone, not heavily blotched, and the nests were scantily lined with bits of dry seaweed, dead grass and the like. The bird itself, in summer plumage, is one of the loveliest waders, with its nicely-patterned black and white head, chestnut patch on the shoulder, and black breast.

It was on the north shore of Store Ekkerøy that I had the intriguing experience of finding an extremely tame turnstone. It seems that in many species of wader a few unusually tame individuals occur, with the frequency varying according to species. The turnstone which allowed me to approach within a few feet while it continued to incubate must surely have been exceptional. I was almost able to touch it before it sidled off its eggs and stood a few feet away, calling 'teeu teeu'. The nest was just above the high water mark, in a situation typical of the ringed plover and oystercatcher, among dried seaweed, pieces of wood, plastic and other flotsam. One could drive the car to within 2 or 3 m of this nest without making the bird leave its eggs, for it was only 10 m from the rough track which follows the Ekkerøy shoreline.

Among the birds of the Varanger shore are a handful of passerines. The rock pipit is found where the coast is rocky, especially on the northern and eastern shores of the peninsula, and the snow bunting haunts the shore in many places. On the now uninhabited island of Lille Ekkerøy, for example, which is rocky in places but very low and mostly grassy, there were 4–6 pairs of snow buntings when I spent the day there on 6 July 1972. One pair was feeding young in a hole in a low cliff just above a group of kittiwakes' nests. Another pair with fledged young frequented the substantial remains of a wooden farmstead – the only remaining sign of the once flourishing human occupation here. They could be seen perching about the roofs of this deserted habitation like so many sparrows. Along the low rocky shore near the north end of the island was another group of fledged young snow buntings. They seemed to belong to two families, because there were eight of them in all. They were charmingly confiding little birds with smoky breasts and whitish eye-rims, and a soft cheeping call not unlike a sparrow's. I watched them for some time as I sat by the shore in the afternoon waiting for the boat from Krampenes to take me back to the mainland. The only other passerines on Lille Ekkerøy were two pairs of pied wagtails with fledged young. Among waders, turnstones, also with young, were prominent; and one or two pairs of redshanks had hatched off their eggs in the abandoned hayfields.

The hay, which begins to grow at the end of May, is cut and heaped on short lengths of fence to dry. This photograph was taken on 15 July, near Nesseby.

Opposite, top: *A magpie's nest at Store Ekkerøy was built on the telephone wires against the wall of a house and constructed mainly of pieces of wire. In this way, this typical village bird has been able to extend its range beyond the limits of tree growth.*

Opposite, bottom: *This magpie was caught by the camera in mid-air as it flew from one fence-post to the next one, near its nest in a low birch tree at Nesseby.*

The hooded crow breeds virtually throughout the Varanger Peninsula. Where trees do not grow it finds substitute trees in the shape (below) *of the navigation light at the entrance to Store Ekkerøy harbour or* (opposite) *of the fish-drying racks at Syltefjord.*

A curlew swoops at a human intruder at Nesseby. Its young are hiding in the hayfield below.

Below: *Ruffs at their lek on the outskirts of the village of Saltjern are surrounded by incubating Arctic terns.* Bottom: *Two ruffs near their lekking-place at Saltjern follow a reeve (left) through the marsh.*

Waders displaying. Below: *On 12 June, on the shore of Store Ekkerøy, a bar-tailed godwit flies after another bird, probably its mate, trilling loudly.* Opposite: *Saltjern, 11 June. A pair of redshanks courting. One bird accompanies the other, trilling loudly and continuously, and rapidly vibrating its raised wings.*

A bar-tailed godwit on the north shore of Store Ekkerøy, a favourite feeding place of these handsome waders.

Opposite, top: *A remarkably tame turnstone which had laid its four eggs just above the high tide line sidles off the nest with depressed tail as the author attempts to touch it.*

Opposite, bottom: *A turnstone's reaction to human invasion of its nesting territory: it stands on a rock and calls loud and long 'wheeter wheeter wheeter'.*

Some woodland birds

10

Genuine birch woodland only exists in the south-western part of the Varanger Peninsula, but birch and willow scrub is found here and there in the river valleys throughout the area, and some of the typical woodland birds, for example the brambling and redwing, inhabit this scrub, which also in places provides a suitable habitat for bluethroats and red-throated pipits. These species have already been mentioned in an earlier chapter; others, such as the song thrush, garden warbler and cuckoo, inhabit the birch forest in the south-western corner of the peninsula, the first two sparsely, the third more commonly, but are familiar enough to need no elaborate description or photograph here. In any case they more or less escaped my attention while I was there. In this chapter a handful of species only will be mentioned; those with which I became most familiar, in particular the fieldfare and redwing, the brambling and redpoll, and the willow tit.

Less than a kilometre north of Vadsø, by the road, or rough track rather, which leads gently upwards towards the fells but then comes to an end, for driving purposes, at some level ground by a waterfall which served me and many another visitor to Vadsø as a camp site, there is a small rectangular birch wood. This, I was told, was Vadsø Park. The trees had curious crooked trunks and many were stunted or contorted in some way, but they had been thickly planted on fertile ground and had become some of the tallest and best-grown birch trees anywhere to be seen in the area. This was surely one of Scandinavia's most north-easterly birch forests. When I paid my first visit to Vadsø Park, on 15 June, I was looking for the fieldfares which Jostein had told me nested here. The trees were still quite leafless though their swollen buds would soon be bursting into leaf. Without difficulty I spotted a substantial nest high in a solid fork of one of these trees: the head of an incubating fieldfare was clearly visible at one side, and its long tail on the other. Other nests were soon found, for the fieldfare breeds in colonies. The nests, and the eggs most of them contained, were very like those of the blackbird: a solid cup of hard mud with straw, dry grass, even string, outside it and finer grass inside for a lining and bluish-green eggs peppered with reddish brown. I had soon found half a dozen occupied nests, two of which contained small young. Most were relatively high up, in situations reminiscent of the mistle thrush, but one was only four feet above the ground.

In the Varanger Peninsula the fieldfare is by no means dependent on trees for its nest sites. At Sandfjord on the north-east coast, far beyond the tree line, there is a flourishing colony nesting both on rocks and on the ground. Near Hanglefjell I found a nest on the support of a bridge and several on a steep high river bank. The fish drying racks which are found by every village offered the most favoured sites of all and enabled the fieldfare to nest, for example, in such treeless places as Berlevåg on the remote north coast of the peninsula. At Hamningberg, and elsewhere beyond the tree-line, the birds nest on houses.

By 26 June, when I had finished building a hide in a birch tree by one of the low fieldfare's nests in Vadsø Park, fledged fieldfares were spluttering about all through the wood, although some nests still only contained eggs. In mine there were now small young, and the adults were visiting the nest at intervals of twenty or thirty minutes. Both birds fed the young with earthworms and, as one of them approached, six quivering open beaks suddenly appeared in the nest, supported on six upstretched necks. I noticed that these still featherless young fieldfares responded to the 'chuck chuck' note of their own parent, but not to those of neighbouring birds. The parent brought up to six worms at a time, which it deposited in the nearest beak, so that one of the young often obtained a large meal while the others got nothing. The last brood of fieldfares in Vadsø Park that I knew of fledged on 15 July, by which time the wood was strangely empty of these large, noisy birds which had been so evident there in mid-June.

While I was in the Varanger Peninsula I had hoped to photograph redwings as well as fieldfares, but I was disappointed. Although redwings were singing everywhere, even in the treeless north-east of the peninsula at places like Sandfjord, and near Hanglefjell, I never succeeded in finding a nest. Yet I searched and searched, in the extensive birch woods near Nyborg, where they were very common; in and around Vadsø Park, where several pairs were evidently breeding; in the wooded Tomaselv valley; and in many other places. I had to remain content with a tape-recording of the singularly melodious but very variable song, which might be rendered 'ee ee jay jay jay chustle'.

Besides the fieldfare colony of about twenty nests there were several pairs of redpolls nesting in Vadsø Park. I found a nest with two well-feathered young, ready to fly, near the top of one of the birches on 26 June; much later, on 15 July, I found another nest in Vadsø Park containing five eggs. This bird returned to its tiny nest of fluff and dry grass while I sat on a branch two metres away. All the time while I was photographing the fieldfares these delightful redpolls were flying to and fro above the tree tops singing their heads off. Although I tried hard to separate the two species of redpoll in the field by noting, in so far as this was possible, the degree of whiteness of their rumps and other characters, I came to the conclusion that there was endless variety, particularly in the amount of white on the back and in the distribution of pink on the head and breast. It really was quite futile to claim to have seen both common and Arctic redpolls; I put them all down as redpolls! Although probably commonest in the wooded areas, the redpoll was the only bird that I saw in virtually every part of the Varanger Peninsula, and it probably is its most widely distributed, and commonest, species.

Another characteristic bird of the Varanger birch woods was the brambling. Its greenfinch-like 'teeze' was to be heard wherever there was a growth of birch or willow scrub, but in the birch forest it was exceedingly common. All the nests I found were very late: one contained four quite well-grown young on 15 July, but another had laid only a single egg on 1 July, and in two other nests the first egg was laid on 26 June. In one of these, the eggs hatched only on 12 July. Apparently this species is a late breeder in the Varanger Peninsula. Bramblings seem to use a high proportion of man-made materials in their nests. One in Vadsø Park was largely built of coloured strips of crepe paper, though lined with feathers; another near Nyborg was held together with cotton. The male brambling in summer plumage, with his black head, reddish upper breast, chestnut back, and white mark on the rump, is a most striking and attractive bird. In the Varanger Peninsula, this species entirely replaces the chaffinch, which is unknown there.

On 22 June I heard the rasping note of a willow tit in Vadsø Park and, after a short search, I found a fledged willow tit, a tiny ball of soft feathers, perched on a birch log. Soon the adult bird called 'chay chay', and I found two more young birds perched on or near the ground. All three were calling repeatedly. The nest was less than a metre above ground, in a hole in a birch stump which had evidently been excavated by the birds. As I examined it a young bird appeared in the hole, looking out, and was soon joined by another. The two stayed there side by side, then one of them suddenly took the plunge and flew off. Almost at once another young tit took its place in the nest entrance, and, when another bird flew, still another appeared in the hole, while I could hear at least one other bird calling inside the stump. It must have been a brood of eight or nine at least that I was lucky enough to see fledging. For an hour afterwards I watched and photographed these tiny fragile creatures as they tried to find secure perches in the high wind that was blowing, and called constantly for food, which the adults busily brought to them.

This brambling's nest in Vadsø Park was constructed partly of string and strips of crepe paper and, as usual in this species, was thickly lined with feathers.

The fieldfares of Vadsø Park. Above: *The author about to enter a hide constructed in one of the park's birch trees. The nest is low down on the left-hand tree.* Opposite: *The adult fieldfare brings a worm for the young.*

A redpoll settles momentarily on a stump near its nest in Vadsø Park. This little bird is probably the commonest and certainly the most widely distributed of all the Varanger Peninsula's birds.

The tiny fragile nest of a redpoll, complete with its complement of eggs, built on the fork of a birch tree in Vadsø Park.

These fledgling willow tits were photographed in Vadsø Park. Opposite: *There was just room for two at a time to perch side by side in the nest-hole entrance before they took their first flight.* Above: *This one has found a secure perch on a fence post but it is as yet extemely unsteady on its feet.*

Hornøy

11 It was a dull cool windy day on 13 July when I made my way at 0800 hours down to the harbour at Vardø to meet the lighthouse keeper who had promised to take me to the island of Hornøy. A few minutes later, clad in waterproofs, we were speeding through the harbour entrance and out into the open sea where the boat, propelled by an outboard motor, crashed its way through the waves, thumping down into each trough with a bone-shaking thud. It was necessary to hold the wooden seat firmly with both hands so as to anchor oneself to it and avoid being thrown into the air. The boatman rode astride, gripping the plank we sat on with his knees: I did the same on the return journey. The journey was short and a jetty with steps made the landing very easy. I was soon struggling upwards towards the top of the island, laden with photograhic equipment.

Hornøy is an exciting place to visit. It is perhaps one of the most interesting and important bird islands not yet subject to the controls and discipline of a nature reserve. Unofficially, however, the lighthouse keepers act as wardens and the high price they charge for the trip over to the island – 100 Norwegian crowns, nearly £6 – may deter visitors. Of course, Hornøy is extremely remote, too. Nonetheless, its flourishing colony of common and Brünnich's guillemots, and its numerous other breeding seabirds, probably ought to be more effectively protected than they are at present.

Hornøy is squarish in outline on the map. It is a rounded hump rising only 67 m above the sea, and its 90 acres constitute the most easterly piece of Norwegian territory. Most of the birds are to be found along the cliffs on the west side which are low and interrupted by hedges and grassy slopes. The vegetation is extraordinarily lush all over the island, in remarkable contrast to the stone wastes of the neighbouring mainland. On the east side especially, where the soil is peaty, there is a rank tall growth of ferns, grass, sorrel and other plants. On the western slopes a cruciferous plant grows in luxuriant abundance and there are marguerites, buttercups, red campions and other flowers in profusion. Presumably some at least of this lush vegetation has been due to fertilisation by the birds. It makes walking about the western cliffs in July mainly a matter of struggling through a thick green mat of the shiny-leaved crucifer above-mentioned. Hereabouts the young gulls, which hatch in great numbers all over the flatter parts of the island in spite of systematic egging, are very easy to find. You would come across a patch of flattened, trampled vegetation with bare earth showing here and there, and almost at once you would spot a couple of grey downy backsides protruding from under the leaves and grass on the edge of this cleared area.

The first more or less ornithological event in Hornøy's history was the landing there on 11 June 1894 of Aubyn Trevor-Battye, a more than usually eccentric Englishman whose successful efforts to get cut off by the ice on Kolguev Island with his manservant were unblushingly described by himself in his book *Ice-bound on Kolguev*. Trevor-Battye's ornithology has been regarded as suspect on two counts: he thought the black-backed gulls on the islands off Vardø were lesser black-backed gulls, whereas now, and surely then too, they are and were greater black-backed gulls. Secondly, he claimed to have seen both common and Brünnich's guillemots breeding on Hornøy, whereas Brünnich's guillemot was not regarded, throughout the first half of the twentieth century, as a breeding bird in Norway, though some nineteenth century writers had recorded it. However, in the summer of 1964 the well-known Norwegian ornithologist and sea-bird expert, Einar Brun, was able to confirm that Brünnich's guillemot was breeding on at least three Norwegian islands: Vedøy in the southern Lofotens; Hjelmsøy, north-east of Hammerfest; and Hornøy. Perhaps Trevor-Battye was right on this point after all?

It seems remarkable that an Arctic species like Brünnich's guillemot should breed as far south as Norway. The colony at Hornøy, like the others, is a mixed one of common and Brünnich's guillemots, and the variety of birds on the breeding ledges is increased by the presence of a quite high proportion of the bridled or spectacled form of the common guillemot. At first, as I scrutinised the breeding sea-birds of Hornøy with binoculars that I could scarcely hold still because of the wind, I despaired of picking out and locating the Arctic species from the common one. It was only after I had clambered closer to the largest group of breeding guillemots that I spotted my first Brünnich's guillemot. I soon learned to distinguish the two species by the Brünnich's guillemots shorter and fatter-looking bill, wider at the base; by its flatter-looking forehead; and by the whitish streak along the bill. Even so, close examination is necessary to separate the two, and a common guillemot with a small fish in its bill could easily be mistaken, at a distance, for a Brünnich's guillemot. I personally would not feel justified, therefore, in accepting the record of one visiting ornithologist I met, of Brünnich's guillemots seen in flight from the jetty at Hamningberg.

On Hornøy, on 13 July, the two species of guillemot had reached a similar stage of development in their breeding cycle. In each species, about half the individuals seemed to have an egg still, and about half had a chick. I was able to establish that at least eighteen Brünnich's guillemots had either a chick or egg, but a good many more birds than this were present. Although there were ledges crowded with guillemots at several points along the western cliffs, in particular at the extreme north-western point, Brünnich's guillemots seemed to be confined to one place only, towards the southern end of these cliffs, where there was a sizeable concentration of common guillemots on sloping rock slabs.

Seldom have I enjoyed an ornithological experience as exciting and moving as those hours I spent on Hornøy. Though there was a freezing wind, and an overcast sky made colour photography almost impossible, I exposed half a dozen black-and-white films in a very short time. Naturally, the Brünnich's guillemots were the main attraction, but other breeding sea-birds could be watched here to perfection. There were shags with young, six or ten pairs I thought; there were razorbills grouped especially on either side of the main guillemot concentration; and puffins swarmed everywhere. As one moved about the slopes the puffins waddled out of their holes in the peaty ground and stood in rows on the projecting ledges gazing at one, ready to take off into safety if necessary, but loath to abandon their nesting burrows. These birds were more approachable here than anywhere else I have seen them. In one burrow I found and examined the first young puffin I have ever seen – a big strong chap, softly downy and warm, dark grey in colour with grey bill and feet. Kittiwakes nested in hundreds wherever the cliffs were sheer, though in many places it was not difficult to walk along below the nests and examine their contents. In one place the heaped-up detritus which had fallen from the kittiwakes' nests and accumulated along the base of the cliff below them was more than a foot thick.

This then was Hornøy. From its summit one looked eastwards over the Barents Sea; but the view from the western slopes extended across the strait to the sister-island of Reinøy, studded all over with breeding gulls and patches of marguerite, and to Vardø on its island and, beyond, to the distant mainland shores and stony slopes of the Varanger Peninsula where I had now spent more than a month.

Hundreds of puffins nest in Hornøy's peaty cliff slopes. When disturbed by a human intruder they crowd onto projecting rocks in readiness for flight. In this photograph the island of Reinøy is on the right, the town of Vardø is on the far left, and the Varanger Peninsula mainland is in the background.

Brünnich's guillemot on Hornøy. Although Brünnich's guillemots are confined to a small section of the area occupied by breeding common guillemots, the two species occur together on the same ledge. Above: *Close-up of a Brünnich's guillemot. This bird's nearest neighbour was a common guillemot.* Opposite: *A single Brünnich's guillemot among common guillemots.*

Brünnich's guillemots and breeding common guillemot sharing the same ledge.

About 30 per cent of Hornøy's guillemots are of the so-called bridled form, having a white ring round the eye and a white line behind it. This bird's chick has only just hatched out, leaving large pieces of egg-shell on either side of it.

Heads of Hornøy's seabirds.
Below: *The razorbill.*
Opposite, top: *The common guillemot.*
Opposite, bottom: *The Brünnich's guillemot. Note the conspicuous white mark at the base of the bill and compare the shape of the bill with that of the common guillemot opposite.*

Guillemots on Hornøy. A general view of part of the main concentration on an area of sloping rock slabs towards the southern end of the island's west coast. The bridled birds are much in evidence here, but there are no Brünnich's guillemots, for these are grouped on the fringe of the auk colony.

Systematic list of the birds of the Varanger Peninsula

This list, which must be regarded as extremely provisional, is based on information in S. Haftorn's book *Norges fugler* (1971), other published records, my own notes (1972), and material supplied by Jostein Grastveit up to the end of 1978. I am much indebted to him for his help.

Red-throated diver, smålom, *Gavia stellata*. Breeds on suitable waters throughout the peninsula, but it was by no means common in 1972. Blair (1936) described it as 'very common'.

Black-throated diver, storlom, *G. arctica*. Breeds, but sparsely only. It must have declined considerably in numbers since Blair (1936) described it as 'very common': I saw none in 1972.

Great northern diver, islom, *G. immer*. A rare visitor. One in winter plumage by Store Ekkerøy, June-July 1970 and another on 6 April 1971. Two at Hamningberg, July 1973.

White-billed diver, gulnebblom, *G. adamsii*. A winter visitor; some individuals summer, mostly in winter plumage.

Slavonian grebe, horndykker, *Podiceps auritus*. Nineteenth-century records from Nyborg and the River Tana only?

Red-necked grebe, gråstrupedykker, *P. griseigena*. A rare visitor.

Fulmar, havhest, *Fulmarus glacialis*. A common winter visitor, staying until May; there are some recent summer records.

Sooty shearwater, grålire, *Puffinus griseus*. One, Vadsøya, 28 November 1971.

Leach's petrel, stormsvale, *Oceanodroma leucorrhoa*. One at Nesseby 7 July, and again on 15 July, 1973.

Gannet, havsule, *Sula bassana*. Since 1961 the colony on the north shore of Syltefjord, on the north-east coast of the peninsula, has increased in size to over twenty breeding pairs. Ninety-one adults were present in July 1973. Has been seen in winter in recent years.

Cormorant, storskarv, *Phalacrocorax carbo*. There are breeding colonies on Store Ekkerøy, the islands off Vardø, Kongsøya (over 100 pairs) and neighbouring islands, and probably elsewhere.

Shag, toppskarv, *P. aristotelis*. Perhaps more widespread than the cormorant, but colonies are smaller. There is one near the head of the Varanger Fjord not far from Nesseby.

Heron, hegre, *Ardea cinera*. An immature bird was shot near Vadsø in autumn, apparently 1938 (Williams, 1941). One at Berlevåg, 15 May 1973.

Purple heron, purpurhegre, *A. purpurea*. A single record, to me doubtful but accepted by Haftorn (1971), of one seen near Krampenes on 24 July 1950 (Taylor, 1953).

Barnacle goose, hvitkinngås, *Branta leucopsis*. A rare passage-migrant; has been recorded in summer.

Brent goose, ringgås, *B. bernicla*. A passage-migrant? One at Storelv, 11 June 1974.

Grey lag goose, gragås, *Anser anser*. A rare passage-migrant; may have bred.

White-fronted goose, tundragås, *A. albifrons*. A flock of 15 flying west at Vestre Jakobselv on 26 June 1971.

Lesser white-fronted goose, dverggås, *A. erythropus*. Bred commonly at least in the southern part of the peninsula, up till the late 1930s. There are no recent breeding records but 2 and 7 individuals were seen near Store Ekkerøy in July 1971.

Bean goose, saedgås, *A. f. fabalis*. It is said to breed above Nesseby and elsewhere in the south of the peninsula, but no breeding records have been published and Blair (1936) never saw this species in the Varanger Peninsula.

Pink-footed goose, kortnebbgås, *A. f. brachyrhynchus*. Rare passage-migrant; one spring record of four near Vadsø in June 1927 (Blair, 1936). Up to 80 recorded in flight north of Vadsø on 1 July 1971.

Mute swan, knoppsvane, *Cygnus olor*. Identified once at Berlevåg; up to 12 swans there in June-July 1973 not specifically identified.

Whooper swan, sangsvane, *C. cygnus*. Has bred on a few occasions but not recorded doing so since a pair nested near Varangerbotn in 1927. Two seen between Vardø and Hamningberg, 9 July 1971.

Bewick's swan, dvergsvane, *C. bewickii*. The first certain record from Norway was one shot at Nesseby, 31 May 1876; but there are no subsequent records from the Varanger Peninsula.

Ruddy shelduck, rustand, *Tadorna ferruginea*. A single (unlikely!) record from Berlevåg: one seen on 2 July 1964.

Shelduck, gravand, *T. tadorna*. There are a handful of very old records from the Varanger Fjord and it has been seen there recently in autumn; for example at Nesseby.

Mallard, stokkand, *Anas platyrhynchos*. There are several summer records from the Varanger Peninsula: it has probably bred. I saw none.

Teal, krikkand, *A. crecca*. Reported by Blair as a common breeder in the 1920s and it no doubt still breeds. I saw this species along the south coast and at Sandfjord in the north-east.

Widgeon, brunnakke, *A. penelope*. A few pairs probably breed regularly in the south-west of the peninsula: I saw a pair on Vadsøya on 20 June.

Pintail, stjertand, *A. acuta*. Probably breeds regularly. I saw it at Nesseby, near Store Ekkerøy, and at the mouth of the River Storelv.

Garganey, knekkand, *A. querquedula*. The first Finnmark record: one shot at Vadsø, 5 September 1972.

Shoveler, skjeand, *A. clypeata*. Several recent summer records from Vadsøya.

Pochard, taffeland, *Aythya ferina*. A single nineteenth-century record from the head of the Varanger Fjord.

Tufted duck, toppand, *A. fuligula*. I saw one in the extreme south-west of the peninsula; it is a regular summer visitor and probably breeds at least in the south-west. One at Vardø, 7 July 1971.

Scaup, bergand, *A. marila*. Scattered pairs evidently breed here and there in the Varanger Peninsula; I saw two pairs a few miles south of Kongsfjord on 16 and 18 June.

Eider, aerfugl, *Somateria mollissima*. Breeds commonly all round the coast, forming large colonies on many of the offshore islands. It is also common in winter.

King eider, praktaerfugl, *S. spectabilis*. A common winter visitor, especially in the Varanger Fjord; up to 1,000 have been seen in Vadsø harbour in the spring and 4,400 were estimated off Vardø on 16 April 1972. A few usually summer, in number varying much from year to year, but breeding has not been proved.

Spectacled eider, brilleaerfugl, *S. fischeri*. A male was shot at Vardø, 12 December 1933.

Steller's eider, Stellers and, *Polysticta stelleri*. A common winter visitor with peak numbers of over 1,000 in some years in the Varanger Fjord in February-April. It is also present annually in summer especially between Nesseby and Vardø, in flocks of up to 100 or more birds, often with drakes predominating. Its status does not seem to have changed substantially since Blair's day. Although young were supposed to have been seen near Vadsø and along the River Storelv in 1924 (Blair, 1936), neither Blair nor anyone else has found a nest.

Common scoter, svartand, *Melanitta nigra*. Breeds at least in the southern half of the peninsula: I saw five on 5 July 1972 on a lake inland from Krampenes.

Velvet scoter, sjoorre, *M. fusca*. Evidently a sparse breeder; c. 20 seen along the Varanger Fjord shore in July 1969.

Surf scoter, brilleand, *M. perspicillata*. One seen at the mouth of the River Tana, 19 September 1970 and again in September 1971 and 1972.

Long-tailed duck, havelle, *Clangula hyemalis*. A common breeding bird which is also present in winter. Up to 1,000 have been seen in April off Vardø.

Goldeneye, kvinand, *Bucephala clangula*. Has been recorded in summer, for example one at Hamningberg in July 1970, but does not breed.

Barrow's goldeneye, Islandsand, *B. islandica*. Two mid-nineteenth century records only.

Smew, Lappfiskand, *Mergus albellus*. Recorded, but only at secondhand, by Blair (1936). At best an occasional visitor only.

Red-breasted merganser, siland, *M. serrator*. A summer visitor which breeds commonly.

Goosander, laksand, *M. merganser*. A very common breeder.

Osprey, fiskeørn, *Pandion haliaetus*. A rare visitor.

Black kite, svartglente, *Milvus migrans*. 1, Syltefjord, 14 July 1973.

Goshawk, hønsehauk, *Accipiter gentilis*. A rare visitor.

Golden eagle, kongeørn, *Aquila chrysaetos*. A rare visitor.

Rough-legged buzzard, fjellvåk, *Buteo lagopus*. A summer visitor which breeds in varying numbers; in some years it is scarce and may not breed at all.

Hen harrier, myrhauk, *Circus cyaneus*. Recorded in July 1924 and summer 1939 when there were two pairs near Vadsø; has been recorded occasionally in the last ten years.

Gyr falcon, jaktfalk, *Falco rusticolus*. A pair or two may breed in the Varanger Peninsula.

Peregrine falcon, vandrefalk, *F. peregrinus*. A few pairs may breed; the last published breeding record was in the Tomaselv Valley, near Vadsø, in 1939.

Merlin, dvergfalk, *F. columbarius*. A common breeding bird at least until the late 1930s, and it was described as common in 1953. I saw none in 1972 and it seems now to be rare.

Kestrel, tårnfalk, *F. tinnunculus*. Occasional summer records from the south, the latest being a pair at Vestre Jakobselv in June 1971. Has certainly bred on occasion.

Willow grouse, lirype, *Lagopus lagopus*. A resident which breeds throughout the lower fells though not very abundantly nowadays.

Ptarmigan, fjellrype, *L. mutus*. Breeds in the higher fells and on lower ground in the northern half of the peninsula, but is nowhere very common.

Crane, trane, *Grus grus*. Said to have been seen near Komagvaer in 1966.

Coot, sothøne, *Fulica atra*. Two nineteenth-century and one or two recent records. For example, one at Vadsøya on 26 June 1973 and one at Nesseby 6 April 1974.

Little bustard, dvergtrappe, *Otis tetrax*. One shot on the Varangerfjord around 1906.

Oystercatcher, tjeld, *Haematopus ostralegus*. A common summer visitor which breeds all round the coast on suitable shores.

Ringed plover, sandlo, *Charadrius hiaticula*. A common shore-breeding summer visitor all round the peninsula. It is also found inland in suitable stony areas.

Caspian plover, rødbrystlo, *C. asiaticus*. One at Ekkerøy, June 1978, the first for Norway.

Dotterel, boltit, *Eudromias morinellus*. Breeds sparsely on the higher fells, especially in the southern half of the peninsula. It seems to be a good deal scarcer than it was in Blair's day (1936).

Golden plover, heilo, *Pluvialis apricaria*. Breeds commonly on suitable peaty or marshy ground throughout the peninsula, up to at least 350 m and down to near sea level. Flocks of up to 40 form in the first half of July.

Grey plover, tundralo, *P. squatarola*. A rare passage-migrant in spring and autumn.

Lapwing, vipe, *Vanellus vanellus*. Two seen at Varangerbotn, 11 July 1971. In more recent years it has been seen every summer and has bred at Nesseby.

Turnstone, steinvender, *Arenaria interpres*. There are breeding colonies along the coast between Vadsø and Vardø as well as inland on stony ground in the lower fells. The eggs I saw were all out in the open in sparsely-lined nests, but Blair found some thickly-built nests, one at least well hidden under a stone.

Little stint, dvergsnipe, *Calidris minutus*. A sparse summer visitor which breeds, or has bred, here and there in a good many places. Has it become more common since Blair worked this area in the 1920s and 1930s? It is surprising that he never found a nest.

Temminck's stint, Temmincksnipe, *C. temminckii*. A common breeder especially in coastal hayfields, and in marshes inland where it is found in loose colonies.

Pectoral sandpiper, Alaskasnipe, *C. melanotus*. A wader thought to be of this species was seen at Store Ekkerøy on 24 June 1964; a definite record from Vadsø, 11 June 1968.

Purple sandpiper, fjaereplytt, *C. maritima*. Present on the shore throughout the year. It breeds here and there in the inland fells.

Dunlin, myrsnipe, *C. alpina*. Breeds commonly throughout the peninsula, especially in the low-lying coastal areas in the south. A common passage-migrant.

Curlew sandpiper, tundrasnipe, *C. ferruginea*. A few records, all in June and July; but recently small flocks have turned up in August.

Knot, Polarsnipe, *C. canutus*. A few spring and early summer records but seen regularly in August in recent years.

Sanderling, sandloper, *C. alba*. A few summer records. Small flocks have been seen recently in August-September.

Ruff, brushane, *Philomachus pugnax*. Breeds on suitable marshy or low-lying grassy terrain throughout the peninsula; probably commonest along the south coast.

Broad-billed sandpiper, fjellmyrløper, *Limicola falcinellus*. Has been reported in summer but there are no definite breeding records.

Short-billed dowitcher, kortnebbet bekkasinsnipe, *Limnodromus griseus*. One identified at Vardø on 6 July 1971 was the first for Norway.

Spotted redshank, sotsnipe, *Tringa erythropus*. It has been seen occasionally in summer and suspected of breeding. I saw one bird only in 1972, on 22 June, flying over the fells above Høvik.

Redshank, rødstilk, *T. totanus*. Breeds commonly, especially in the hayfields, on suitable terrain near the coast. Nor is it confined to the Varanger Fjord shore, for it was present at Syltefjord in 1972.

Greenshank, gluttsnipe, *T. nebularia*. A few pairs may breed in the extreme west and south-west of the peninsula, along the River Tana.

Wood sandpiper, grønnstilk, *T. glareola*. Probably breeds in suitable terrain throughout the peninsula; it is quite common between Vadsø and the mouth of the River Storelv.

Common sandpiper, strandsnipe, *T. hypoleucos*. Scattered pairs probably breed on most of the rivers: I saw birds in 1972 near Sandfjord and Syltefjord.

Black-tailed godwit, svarthalespove, *Limosa limosa*. Two recent records from the Vadsø area.

Bar-tailed godwit, lappspove, *L. lapponica*. A common passage-migrant which may breed: birds, sometimes paired, have been seen on several inland marshes in June or July but there are no definite breeding records.

Curlew, storspove, *Numenius arquata*. Breeds in hayfields along the south coast of the peninsula and probably elsewhere; heard calling near Syltefjord, 23 June 1972.

Whimbrel, småspove, *N. phaeopus*. A common breeder on the lower fells of the southern half of the peninsula.

Little whimbrel, dvergspove, *N. borealis*. One near Hamningberg, 14 July 1969, Europe's first.

Snipe, enkeltbekkasin, *Gallinago gallinago*. Breeds commonly on suitable grounds, probably throughout the peninsula.

Great snipe, dobbeltbekkasin, *G. media*. There are three recent summer records of single birds seen, and a nest was found near Krampenes on 17 June 1938.

Jack snipe, kvartbekkasin, *Lymnocryptes minimus*. It has been heard in song flight over marshes in the south and west of the peninsula. Apparently no nests have been found since the 1920s and 1930s, when Blair and others found several in the neighbourhood of Vadsø.

Red-necked phalarope, svømmesnipe, *Phalaropus lobatus*. Beeds commonly in suitable places throughout the peninsula. Flocks of up to 100 or more are present along the south coast in summer.

Grey phalarope, Polarsvømmesnipe, *P. fulicarius*. One ringed at Vadsøya, 10 August 1970; a few other records in recent years, June-November.

Great skua, storjo, *Stercorarius skua*. Seen every summer in recent years.

Pomarine skua, Polarjo, *S. pomarinus*. A passage-migrant which sometimes appears in numbers in the Varanger Fjord in June-August.

Arctic skua, tyvjo, *S. parasiticus*. A common breeder throughout the peninsula, from sea level to the higher fells inland.

Long-tailed skua, fjelljo, *S. longicaudus*. In some years it breeds commonly on the fells inland; in others birds are present without breeding.

Little gull, dvergmåke, *Larus minutus*. One, Nesseby, 11 June 1972. Has also been seen at Vadsø.

Black-headed gull, hettemåke, *L. ridibundus*. There have been a number of summer records in the last ten years and breeding has now been recorded at Nesseby.

Lesser black-backed gull, sildemåke, *L. fuscus*. Recorded near Vadsø in summer 1923 (two individuals) and again in summer 1924, by Blair, and there are some recent summer records.

Herring gull, gråmåke, *L. argentatus*. Breeds commonly round the coast forming large colonies on certain offshore islands like Kongsøya and Hornøy and Reinøy.

Iceland gull, Gronlandsmåke, *L. glaucoides*. This species has been reported on several occasions, and Blair claims to have found a wing near Vadsø in June 1925. Two, Berlevåg, 15 July 1973.

Glaucous gull, Polarmåke, *L. hyperboreus*. A winter visitor and a regular summer visitor in small numbers. On 24 March 1964 there were over 300 in Vardø harbour.

Great black-backed gull, svartbak, *L. marinus*. Breeds commonly round the coast, often in mixed colonies with herring gulls.

Common gull, fiskemåke, *L. canus*. A common inland and coastal breeder.

Sabine's gull, Sabinemåke, *L. sabini*. One over the Varangerfjord, 14 August 1971.

Kittiwake, krykkje, *Rissa tridactyla*. There are breeding colonies at Store Ekkerøy, Lille Ekkerøy, Vardø, Hornøy, Reinøy, Syltefjord, Kongsøya and doubtless elsewhere.

Ross's gull, Rosenmåke, *Rhodostethia rosea*. One shot in the Syltefjord, 28 May 1938.

Ivory gull, ismåke, *Pagophila eburnea*. One shot at Hamningberg, May 1883.

Black tern, svartterne, *Chlidonias nigra*. One at Nesseby along the Varangerfjord, 7 July 1973.

Common tern, makrellterne, *Sterna hirundo*. Has been recorded and may breed.

Arctic tern, rødnebbterne, *S. paradisea*. There are numerous breeding colonies throughout the peninsula, chiefly near the coasts.

Little auk, alkekonge, *Plotus alle*. A winter visitor.

Razorbill, alke, *Alca torda*. Breeds at Kongsøya, Syltefjord, Reinøy, Hornøy, possibly Store Ekkerøy, and elsewhere.

Guillemot, lomvi, *Uria aalge*. Breeds in some numbers at Syltefjord and on Reinøy and Hornøy.

Brünnich's guillemot, Polarlomvi, *U. lomvia*. Has bred in increasing numbers with guillemots on Hornøy and at Syltefjord at least since 1964–6.

Black guillemot, teiste, *Cepphus grylle*. Breeds on a number of offshore islands, including Kongsøya, Hornøy and Store Ekkerøy.

Puffin, lunde, *Fratercula arctica*. Breeds on Kongsøya, at Syltefjord, and on Hornøy and Reinøy, and perhaps elsewhere. All colonies appear to be small; the largest is probably Hornøy.

Collared dove, Tyrkerdue, *Streptopelia decaocto*. Seen recently at Vadsø.

Turtle dove, turteldue, *S. turtur*. One shot recently, Hamningberg.

Cuckoo, gjøk, *Cuculus canorus*. Common in the birch woods of the south-west of the peninsula.

Snowy owl, snøugle, *Nyctea scandiaca*. A few pairs probably breed, perhaps not every year, in the fells inland. No nest has apparently ever been found in the Varanger Peninsula.

Short-eared owl, jordugle, *Asio flammeus*. Has frequently been seen in the southern half of the peninsula and probably breeds.

Hawk owl, haukugle, *Surnia ulula*. Said to have bred 'commonly' some years ago.

Ural owl, slagugle, *Strix uralensis*. One shot at Varangerbotn, 2 April 1964.

Great grey owl, Lappugle, *S. nebulosa*. Specimens were secured in the Vadsø district in autumn 1938 (Williams, 1941).

Swift, tårnsvale, *Apus apus*. A few records only.

Roller, blåråke, *Coracias garrulus*. One, Nyborg, October 1868.

Hoopoe, haerfugl, *Upupa epops*. Two old records of birds shot, both in September.

Great spotted woodpecker, flaggspett, *Dendrocopos major*. One shot, Mortensnes, September 1873; remains found on Reinøy and at Skallelv in 1964 and 1967.

Lesser spotted woodpecker, dvergspett, *D. minor*. Breeds in the birch woods in the south-west.

Three-toed woodpecker, tretåspett, *Picoides tridactylus*. A rare visitor.

Sand martin, sandsvale, *Riparia riparia*. There are a few small breeding colonies on the south coast, one being at the mouth of the Maskelv River. A pair nested in 1971 as far east as the Storelv near Ekkerøy. In June 1882 three were seen at Vardø.

Swallow, låvesvale, *Hirundo rustica*. There are many summer records, but breeding in the peninsula has apparently not yet been proved.

House martin, taksvale, *Delichon urbica*. Recorded in summer. Breeding has been reported but needs substantiation.

Shorelark, fjellerke, *Eremophila alpestris*. Breeds commonly along the south coast down to sea level and inland on the coastal fells.

Crested lark, topplerke, *Galerida cristata*. One near Store Ekkerøy, 16 May 1926.

Skylark, lerke, *Alauda arvensis*. A common breeder in the coastal hayfields throughout the peninsula.

Tree pipit, trepiplerke, *Anthus trivialis*. Probably breeds in the birch woods of the south-west.

Meadow pipit, heipiplerke, *A. pratensis*. A common breeder throughout the peninsula in suitable terrain.

Red-throated pipit, Lapp-piplerke, *A. cervinus*. Breeds here and there in suitable habitats throughout the peninsula; commonest near the coast.

Rock pipit, skjaerpiplerke, *A. spinoletta*. Breeds round the coast wherever there are cliffs, but it is by no means common.

Yellow wagtail, gulerle, *Motacilla flava*. Has certainly bred in the southern coastal region in the past and may still do so, though I did not see it in 1972.

Grey wagtail, vintererle, *M. cinerea*. A pair by the Jakobselv River in July 1924 was reported by Blair at second hand; but a bird with juveniles has been seen since then.

White wagtail, linerle, *M. alba*. Breeds commonly throughout the peninsula. One at Vadsø, 3 November 1967.

Red-backed shrike, tornskate, *Lanius collurio*. There are two recent autumn records from near Vadsø: 22–5 August 1968 and 7 October 1972.

Great grey shrike, varsler, *L. excubitor*. Has been seen in summer but breeding has apparently not been substantiated.

Starling, staer, *Sturnus vulgaris*. Was reported breeding at Vardø in 1881 but was unknown in the peninsula for many years thereafter until, in recent years, it has bred at Båtsfjord, Komagvaer, Nyborg, Nesseby and elsewhere.

Nutcracker, nøttekråke, *Nucifraga caryocatactes*. Has been shot in Hamningberg.

Siberian jay, lavskrike, *Perisoreus infaustus*. Common in the south-west of the peninsula, extending east to Vadsø.

Magpie, skjaere, *Pica pica*. A common resident.

Rook, kornkråke, *Corvus frugilegus*. One, Vardø, 1894.

Hooded crow, kråke, *C. corone cornix*. A common resident.

Raven, ravn, *C. corax*. A common resident which breeds round the coast. I surprised 35 in the early morning of 15 July 1972 on the low cliffs of Vadsøya.

Waxwing, sidensvans, *Bombycilla garrulus*. Several seen at Vadsø in January 1968. An occasional visitor.

Dipper, *Cinclus cinclus*. Breeds on suitable streams.

Dunnock, jernspurv, *Prunella modularis*. It has been seen in summer at two places on the north coast and probably breeds there, as well as in the birch woods of the south-west.

Sedge warbler, sivsanger, *Acrocephalus schoenobaenus*. A local summer visitor which evidently breeds here and there in suitable places.

Garden warbler, hagesanger, *Sylvia borin*. A local summer visitor which probably breeds regularly, especially in the south-west and along the River Tana.

Blackcap, munk, *S. atricapilla*. Four at Vadsø, October 1970.

Willow warbler, løvsanger, *Phylloscopus trochilus*. Common in all suitable areas.

Chiffchaff, gransanger, *P. collybita*. Has been heard singing along the River Tana and at Vadsø, where it was recorded on 27 April 1969 and 19 May 1973.

Arctic warbler, Lappsanger, *P. borealis*. Not seen by me in 1972. In spite of Taylor's report of it in the Varanger Peninsula in 1953, its status remains uncertain.

Goldcrest, fuglekonge, *Regulus regulus*. Recorded in April 1853 and May 1895; also occasionally in recent years in May-September. Two were seen at Vadsø on 23 April 1973.

Pied flycatcher, svarthvit fluesnapper, *Ficedula hypoleuca*. Breeds in the south-west and perhaps elsewhere in the birch zone.

Spotted flycatcher, grå fluesnapper, *Muscicapa striata*. A rare visitor.

Whinchat, buskskvett, *Saxicola rubetra*. Nested at Nesseby, 1967; the only record so far.

Wheatear, steinskvett, *Oenanthe oenanthe*. Breeds commonly, especially in the southern half of the peninsula from sea level up to the higher fells.

Redstart, rødstjert, *Phoenicurus phoenicurus*. Has been recorded in summer on several occasions but breeding has not yet been proved, except apparently at Vardø.

Robin, rødstrupe, *Erithacus rubecula*. One at Vadsø, 12 May 1971.

Bluethroat, blåstrupe, *Luscinia svecica*. Breeds commonly in all suitable habitats.

Fieldfare, gråtrost, *Turdus pilaris*. Breeds colonially throughout the peninsula in trees, on cliffs, on buildings and on the ground.

Ring ouzel, ringtrost, *T. torquatus*. Rather uncommon but may breed.

Blackbird, svarttrost, *T. merula*. A few records only. One at Vadsø, 14 May 1974.

Redwing, rødvingetrost, *T. iliacus*. A common breeder, especially in the birch woods of the south-west; but it is found in willow scrub and other suitable habitats throughout the peninsula.

Song thrush, måltrost, *T. philomelos*. Has been heard on several occasions singing in summer in the birch woods of the south-west and probably breeds there regularly.

Long-tailed tit, stjertmeis, *Aegithalos caudatus*. A rare autumn visitor. Fifteen were seen at Suki near Nesseby on 16 October 1973.

Willow tit, granmeis, *Parus montanus*. Breeds in the birch woods at least as far east as Vadsø.

Siberian tit, Lappmeis, *P. cinctus*. A breeding bird in the birch woods of the south-west though not very common.

Coal tit, svartmeis, *P. ater*. Two nineteenth-century records only.

Great tit, kjottmeis, *P. major*. One was seen at Vadsø in July 1958. It now breeds and has even overwintered in the peninsula.

House sparrow, gråspurv, *Passer domesticus*. Breeds in or near human settlements throughout the peninsula, having apparently colonised the area since about 1930.

Tree sparrow, pilfink, *P. montanus*. In the late nineteenth century there was a flourishing but temporary breeding colony at Nesseby; and breeding was proved at Nyborg, at Vardø and at Gamvik. I did not see this species in 1972 but it bred at Saltjern in 1974 and four young were ringed there on 11 July.

Brambling, bjørkefink, *Fringilla montifringilla*. Widespread and common in all suitable localities, even in the north-east. It occurs in willow or birch scrub as well as birch forest.

Chaffinch, bokfink, *F. coelebs*. A rare visitor; has been seen at Nesseby and Vadsø. All records are in April–May.

Twite, bergirisk, *Acanthis flavirostris*. Scattered birds have been recorded in the last thirty years, but breeding has not been substantiated. Blair does not mention it. Its status needs expert investigation.

Redpoll, gråsisik, *A. flammea*. Very common indeed throughout the peninsula, many birds showing the characteristics of *A. hornemanni*.

Pine grosbeak, konglebit, *Pinicola enucleator*. Has been recorded from Leirpollen and Vadsø.

Crossbill, grankorsnebb, *Loxia curvirostra*. Nine birds, probably of this species, flew east near Vadsø, 19 July 1966.

Two-barred crossbill, båndkorsnebb, *L. leucoptera*. Three or four were seen at Skallelv coming in from the east over the sea on 11 July 1972.

Yellowhammer, gulspurv, *Emberiza citrinella*. Has been seen in various places in the peninsula in recent years but breeding has not yet been proved.

Little bunting, dvergspurv, *E. pusilla*. Two seen on Falkefjell, 1 July 1971.

Rustic bunting, vierspurv, *E. rustica*. One seen near Vadsø, 26 May 1968.

Reed bunting, sivspurv, *E. schoeniclus*. Breeds throughout the peninsula in suitable terrain, but local. Not mentioned there by Blair.

Lapland bunting, Lappspurv, *Calcarius lapponicus*. A common breeder in the bogs and peaty areas, at all levels up to 300 m.

Snow bunting, snøspurv, *Plectrophenax nivalis*. Breeds commonly in stony terrain throughout the peninsula, but is confined in the south-west to the higher tops.

Literature

BERONKA, J. 1933. Vadsø bys historie. Vadsø.
HELLAND, A. 1905. Topografisk-statistisk beskrivelse over Finmarkens Amt. 3 vols. Kristiania.
Norge, Bind 3. 1963. Oslo.
YTREBERG, N. A. 1942. Handelsteder i Finnmark. Trondheim.

ANDERSSON, G. 1971. Dvärgspov, *Numenius minutus*, i Finnmark. Sterna 10: 63-4.
BAYLISS-SMITH, S. 1970. Wild wings to the Northlands. London.
BLAIR, H. M. S. 1936. On the birds of East Finnmark. Ibis (13) 6: 280-308, 429-59 and 651-74.
BRUN, E. 1965. Polarlomvien, *Uria lomvia* (L), som rugefugl i Norge. Sterna 6: 229-50.
BRUN, E. 1967. Hekking av havsule, *Sula bassana*, i Nord-Norge. Sterna 7: 376-86.
BRUN, E. 1969. Utbredelse og hekkebestand av alke (*Alca torda*) i Norge. Sterna 8: 345-59.
BRUN, E. 1969. Utbredelse og hekkebestand av lomvi (*Uria aalge*) i Norge. Sterna 8: 209-24.
BRUN, E. 1970. Dimorph-ratio cline of bridled guillemots (*Uria aalge*) in Norway. Astarte. Journal of Arctic biology 3: 45-50.
DONAHUE, M. and others. 1966. Ornithological observations in Finnmark in the summer of 1962 and 1964. Sterna 7: 121-32.
FERGUSON-LEES, I. J. 1969. Studies of less familiar birds. Little stint. British Birds 62: 382 and Plates 57-9.
GJØSAETER, J. and others. 1972. Dykkender beiter på loddeegg. Sterna 11: 173-5.
GOODERS, J. 1970. Where to watch birds in Britain and Europe. London.
GRASTVEIT, J. 1971. Stellers and ved Vadsø. Sterna 10: 31-4.
HAFTORN, S. 1971. Norges fugler. Oslo.
HAGEN, Y. 1965. Litt om fuglefaunaen i Finnmark og Troms. Sterna 6: 321-49.
ISAKSON, E. 1964. Sommarobservationer i Finnmark. Sterna 6: 297-300.
JENNING, W. 1966. Sommarobservationer i Finnmark, 1965. Sterna 7: 133-4.
KUHN, M. and others. 1973. Kurzschnabel-Schlammläufer *Limnodromos griseus* und andere Beobachtungen während einer Finnmark-Exkursion von 1 bis 13 July 1971. Sterna 12: 65-7.
LØVENSKIOLD, H. L. 1947. Håndbok over Norges fugler. Oslo.
LUNDEVALL, C. F. 1968. Havsulan nordnorsk häckfågel. Fauna och Flora 63: 214-16.
MARTINS, H. 1958. Svarttrost og låvesvale i Vardø. Sterna 3: 189-90.
REYNOLDS, J. F. 1972. Little stint incubating eight eggs. British Birds 65: 526.
RISBERG, E. L. 1972. Fågelobservationer i Varangerområdet, 1966-1971. Sterna 11: 81-95.
SANDGREN, L. 1975. Fågelobservationer i Varangerområdet Juli 1973. Sterna 14: 130.
SCHAANING, H. T. L. 1907. Østfinmarkens fuglefauna. Bergens Mus. Aarb. 8: 1-98.
SCHMIDT, G. 1967. Die Vögel dreier kleiner norwegischer Inseln am Nordmeer. Bonn Zoologische Beiträge 18: 173-98.
SILLS, N. 1971. Beyond the Arctic circle. Birds 3: 3-5.
SJOBERG, K. 1971. Fåglar på Varangerhalvön, Juli 1969. Fauna och Flora 65: 55-61.
TAYLOR, R. J. F. 1953. Notes on the birds of Finnmark. Sterna 1 (10): 3-36.
TREVOR-BATTYE, A. 1895. Ice-bound on Kolguev. London.
WADEN, K. AND HJALTE, K. 1965. Sommarobservationer i Finnmark. Sterna 6: 296.
WATSON, A. 1954. Bridled guillemots in Norway. Bird study 1: 169-73.
WILLIAMS, J. G. 1941. On the birds of the Varanger Peninsula, East Finnmark. Ibis (14) 5: 245-64.